MUIRHEAD LIBRARY OF PHILOSOPHY

An admirable statement of the aims of the Library of Philosophy was provided by the first editor, the late Professor J. H. Muirhead, in his description of the original programme printed in Erdmann's *History of Philosophy* under the date 1890. This was slightly modified in subsequent volumes to take the form of the following statement:

'The Muirhead Library of Philosophy was designed as a contribution to the History of Modern Philosophy under the heads: first of different Schools of Thought—Sensationalist, Realist, Idealist, Intuitivist; secondly of different Subjects—Psychology, Ethics, Aesthetics, Political Philosophy, Theology. While much had been done in England in tracing the course of evolution in nature, history, economics, morals and religion, little had been done in tracing the development of thought on these subjects. Yet "the evolution of opinion is part of the whole evolution". .

'By the co-operation of different writers in carrying out this plan it was hoped that a thoroughness and completeness of treatment, otherwise unattainable, might be secured. It was believed also that from writers mainly British and American fuller consideration of English Philosophy than it had hitherto received might be looked for. In the earlier series of books containing, among others, Bosanquet's *History of Aesthetic*, Pfleiderer's *Rational Theology since Kant*, Albee's *History of English Utilitarianism*, Bonar's *Philosophy and Political Economy*, Brett's *History of Psychology*, Ritchie's *Natural Rights*, these objects were to a large extent effected.

'In the meantime original work of a high order was being produced both in England and America by such writers as Bradley, Stout, Bertrand Russell, Baldwin, Urban, Montague, and others, and a new interest in foreign works, German, French and Italian, which had either become classical or were attracting public attention, had developed. The scope of the Library thus became extended into something more international, and it is entering on the fifth decade of its existence in the hope that it may contribute to that mutal understanding between countries which is so pressing a need of the present time.'

The need which Professor Muirhead stressed is no less pressing today, and few will deny that philosophy has much to do with enabling us to meet it, although no one, least of all Muirhead himself, would regard that as the sole, or even the main, object of philosophy. As

Professor Muirhead continues to lend the distinction of his name to the Library of Philosophy it seemed not inappropriate to allow him to recall us to these aims in his own words. The emphasis on the history of thought also seemed to me very timely; and the number of important works promised for the Library in the very near future augur well for the continued fulfilment, in this and other ways, of the expectations of the original editor.

H. D. LEWIS

MUIRHEAD LIBRARY OF PHILOSOPHY

General Editor: H. D. Lewis

Professor of History and Philosophy of Religion in the University of London

Action by SIR MALCOLM KNOX
The Analysis of Mind by BERTRAND RUSSELL
Belief by H. H. PRICE
Brett's History of Psychology edited by R. S. PETERS
Clarity is Not Enough by H. D. LEWIS
Coleridge as a Philosopher by J. H. MUIRHEAD
The Commonplace Book of G. E. Moore edited by C. LEWY
Contemporary American Philosophy edited by C. P. ADAMS and W. P. MONTAGUE
Contemporary British Philosophy first and second Series edited by J. H. MUIRHEAD
Contemporary British Philosophy third Series edited by H. D. LEWIS
Contemporary Indian Philosophy edited by RADHAKRISHNAN and J. H. MUIRHEAD 2nd edition
Contemporary Philosophy in Australia edited by ROBERT BROWN and C. D. ROLLINS
The Discipline of the Cave by J. N. FINDLAY
Doctrine and Argument in Indian Philosophy by NINIAN SMART
Essays in Analysis by ALICE AMBROSE
Ethics by NICOLAI HARTMANN translated by STANTON COIT 3 vols
The Foundations of Metaphysics in Science by ERROL E. HARRIS
Freedom and History by H. D. LEWIS
The Good Will: A Study in the Coherence Theory of Goodness by H. J. PATON
Hegel: A Re-examination by J. N. FINDLAY
Hegel's Science of Logic translated by W. H. JOHNSTON and L. G. STRUTHERS 2 vols
History of Aesthetic by B. BOSANQUET 2nd edition
History of English Utilitarianism by E. ALBEE
History of Psychology by G. S. BRETT edited by R. S. PETERS abridged one volume edition 2nd edition
Human Knowledge by BERTRAND RUSSELL
A Hundred Years of British Philosophy by RUDOLF METZ translated by J. N. HARVEY, T. E. JESSOP, HENRY STURT
Hypothesis and Perception by ERROL E. HARRIS
Ideas: A General Introduction to Pure Phenomenology by EDMUND HUSSERL translated by W. R. BOYCE GIBSON
Identity and Reality by EMILE MEYERSON
Imagination by E. J. FURLONG

Muirhead Library of Philosophy

EDITED BY H. D. LEWIS

IN CONTACT WITH THE PHYSICAL WORLD

IN CONTACT WITH
THE PHYSICAL WORLD

BY

JOHN PENNYCUICK

M.A., D.Phil.

LONDON · GEORGE ALLEN & UNWIN LTD
NEW YORK · HUMANITIES PRESS INC.

British ISBN 0 04 121015 8

U.S.A. SBN 391–00175–2

Printed in Great Britain
in 12 on 13pt. Barbou type
by W & J Mackay & Co Ltd,
Fair Row, Chatham, Kent

TO LUCY

PREFACE

Few problems have fascinated and absorbed philosophers over the centuries as have those concerning our perception of the physical world. From Descartes onwards, all the most acute philosophical brains have been impelled to attempt their solution. The doctrines they have propounded have been rich in insights, yet none has come near to universal acceptance. Persistently, those which if sound would most fully resolve the theoretical dilemmas have been precisely those which, to an educated layman, appear most far-fetched. While those that he finds credible have most signally failed to come to terms with these dilemmas. For myself, I have always felt that the correct account must be one that is free from both these limitations. To present such an account has been my aim in this book.

Sections I and II pose the problems, against the background of attempts in recent years to dismiss them as fictitious; Section III examines one widely held position that I find untenable; the remaining three sections set forth my own views.

The facts of perception are infinitely complex; but I have limited my enquiry to those I regard as of central importance from a philosophical standpoint. There is a constant danger, in a work of this kind, of one's major contentions being lost from view through a plethora of detail. I am content to leave to others the working out of such detail. If I have on occasion been led to oversimplify, this may be all for the best.

I would like it to be known how much I owe to my former teacher, Sir Alfred Ayer. His empiricist approach has been the target of much criticism in the latter part of this book. But it is he above all, by his meticulous rigour and precision in applying it, who has forced me to crystallize my conflicting point of view. I have to thank too Professor William Kneale, also my teacher, who came to my rescue when I was brought to a standstill by a difficult passage; Professor H. D. Lewis for his unstinted kindness and encouragement, and for drawing attention to several ambiguities that I have sought to clarify; and my distinguished friend Professor

H. H. Price, who painstakingly read over all I had written and made fertile suggestions and comments. I should be wanting in gratitude were I not to mention also the help that was given me by my friend Charlie Parkes, and above all by my mother and father.

JOHN PENNYCUICK

Maids Moreton, Buckingham
October 1970

The author is indebted to the undermentioned for their kindness in allowing quotations from the works cited.

Mr A. A. Kassman, editor of the Aristotelian Society; H. P. Grice, 'The Causal Theory of Perception' (*A. S. Supplementary Proceedings*, 1961)

Macmillan & Co. Ltd and St Martin's Press, Inc. (New York): A. J. Ayer, *The Problem of Knowledge*

Oxford University Press: J. L. Austin, *Sense and Sensibilia*

Routledge & Kegan Paul Ltd and Humanities Press, Inc. (New York): D. M. Armstrong, *Perception and the Physical World*

CONTENTS

It is the recurring misfortune of philosophers to be misunderstood. I dare not hope to escape this; but a word is in place which may help to reduce it.

Those who have so kindly read this work have been repeatedly misled through insufficient attention to what I say in the footnotes. I alone am to blame. Too often—in a desire for continuity in the flow of my argument—I have relegated to the bottom of the page points of vital import deserving mention in the text.

I must therefore beg the reader to give to these points his full consideration.

I

IS THERE A PHILOSOPHICAL PROBLEM
OF PERCEPTION?

It is nowadays frequently held by philosophers that the 'problem of perception' is a bogus one. The reason for this is that the problem cannot really be stated in the first place until one has accepted a certain time-honoured *dichotomy* the validity of which has now come to be widely disputed. This is the dichotomy between physical or 'material' objects and 'sense-data'. Many philosophers have held that in perception what we are directly aware of is never a physical object, such as a table or a book, but always a thing of a different kind generally known as a 'sense-datum'. This being so, they have seen themselves to be faced with two interrelated problems: on the one hand, that of specifying the relationship between sense-data and physical objects[1] and on the other, that of showing what (if any) justification we have for believing that there *are* any physical objects[2] if these are never directly perceived. The main reason for holding this view is provided by the so-called 'argument from illusion'. This argument can be stated as follows.

There are, as anyone would admit, occasions on which we perceive things other than as they really are, occasions on which what we perceive looks, feels or otherwise 'appears' other than it is. The examples most commonly cited include the round coin which looks elliptical from certain points of view and the straight stick which looks bent when partially submerged in water. There are, as well, occasions of complete hallucination where we seem to be perceiving something that does not exist at all.

[1] In other words, that of stating what is involved in perceiving physical objects, assuming that these can still be said to be perceived *indirectly*: In order for a given object to be said to be perceived by a given person, in what way(s) must it be related to what he perceives directly?

[2] Or at any rate that there are physical objects of those particular kinds which, on the authority of our senses, we take there to be.

On such occasions, it cannot be said that what we *directly* perceive or are aware of is a physical object. There is nevertheless *something* of which we *are* directly aware, something whose presence cannot be conjured away and which really does possess that property or set of properties which erroneously appears to be possessed by a physical object. And a thing of this non-physical kind is given the name of 'sense-datum'. Thus, to take the example of the straight stick that looks bent when part of it is in water, what we are directly conscious of is something which really is bent—which, however, cannot be a physical object since there *is* no physical object before us which actually is bent. And it is therefore said to be a 'sense-datum'. Likewise, when, for instance, a D.T.s sufferer 'sees' a pink rat, while there is no (real) pink rat for him to be conscious of, there is nevertheless *something* pink and rat-shaped of which he *is* conscious—which again is said to be a 'sense-datum'.

There seems, however, at first glance, no objection to supposing that when we both really perceive some object (i.e. when the object in question is 'there' to be perceived) and perceive it as it really is—when, for instance, we see a stick which both looks and is bent—then in that case what we perceive directly *is* a physical object, e.g. a stick. But we find, on reflection, that *whether or not* what we are perceiving is in all respects as it perceptually appears to be, and whether or not we are really perceiving it, the actual character of our perceptual experience is, essentially, exactly the same. Thus the kind of experience we have when we are viewing a straight stick which looks bent is essentially the same as if we were viewing one which really was bent. Equally, the kind of experience we have when we only seem to be seeing some object is the same as if we really were seeing it. And this is not what we should expect if in the one case what we are directly perceiving were a physical object, while in the other it were something of an entirely different kind: given a complete difference in the kind of thing of which we are directly conscious, we should expect a corresponding difference in the kind of experience we are having. It seems, therefore, to follow that what we are directly perceiving —the *immediate object* of our perceptual awareness—must actually be a thing of the same kind in both cases. Given, therefore, that in the one case it is a 'sense-datum' which we are directly perceiving, the same must be true in the other also.[1] And thus we reach the conclusion that what we directly perceive is *never* a physical object but always a sense-datum.

That this argument, and hence its conclusion, has now fallen into wide disrepute is due in large part to a short book by the late Professor J. L. Austin entitled *Sense and Sensibilia*.[2] Let us see now what some of his main objections to it are.

He considers that one of the chief stumbling-blocks in this argument lies in its use of the expression 'directly perceive'. How, he asks, might we use the word 'directly' coupled with a verb of perception in ordinary, everyday discourse?

Well, we might, he says, 'contrast the man who saw the procession directly with the man who saw it *through a periscope*; or we might contrast the place from which you can watch the door directly with the place from which you can see it only *in the mirror*. *Perhaps* we might contrast seeing you directly with seeing, say, your shadow on the blind; and *perhaps* we might contrast hearing the music directly with hearing it relayed outside the concert-hall.'[3] However, the 'perhaps' of these last two examples

[1] It has been further pointed out that sometimes there may be literally only an infinitesimal difference in the character of our experience between a case where we perceive something other than as it is and a case where we perceive the very same thing in all respects as it is. Thus, to use Professor H. H. Price's example (*Perception*, Methuen 1932, p. 32), when we see a cricket ball at a distance of twenty yards, it looks flat due to perspective; but if we walk slowly towards it, it begins at a certain distance gradually to unflatten until eventually, namely when it first enters the range of distances from our eyes within which objects are seen in perfect stereoscopy, the shape it looks corresponds exactly with the shape it is. If we now move back again an infinitesimal distance (as short a distance as we please), it will flatten again, but only infinitesimally; and therefore our perceptual experience will undergo only an infinitesimal alteration in character. Are we to say, however, that an infinitesimal alteration in the character of our experience has brought with it a *radical* alteration in the character of what we are directly perceiving, the thing of which we are directly conscious? It would seem that this is plainly impossible; for surely to describe what sort of thing we are directly conscious of is precisely to describe what sort of experience we are having.

[2] Oxford University Press, 1962. This book is a reconstruction by Mr G. J. Warnock from the manuscript notes.

[3] *Sense and Sensibilia*, pp. 15–16.

suggests to Austin that 'the notion of not perceiving "directly" seems most at home where, as with the periscope and the mirror, it retains its link with the notion of a kink in *direction*. It seems that we must not be looking *straight at* the object in question'. And he goes on to say that 'the notion of indirect perception is not naturally at home with senses other than sight', since with them 'there is nothing quite analogous with the "line of vision"'. And 'for this reason alone there seems to be something badly wrong with the question, "Do we perceive things directly or not?", where perceiving is evidently intended to cover the employment of *any* of the senses'.

The conclusion which he draws from these considerations is that, whatever may be the philosopher's use of the words 'directly perceive', it is certainly not 'the ordinary, or any familiar, use'. For it differs from that use in certain quite fundamental respects.

We should ordinarily qualify a verb of perception with the word '*in*directly' only to describe certain special, abnormal cases of perceiving something, and then with the express purpose of indicating that they *were* abnormal in some particular way, e.g. that we saw something not in the way one usually sees things, but through a periscope. And even in this case, we should have to explain that this was what we meant by saying that we had seen it 'indirectly'. As Austin says, 'we always prefer in practice what might be called the *cash-value* expression to the "indirect" metaphor. If I were to report that I see enemy ships indirectly, I should merely provoke the question what exactly I mean. "I mean that I can see these blips on the radar screen"—"Well, why didn't you say so then?"'[1] The word 'directly' itself would serve a useful purpose only in cases where there was some special reason why we *might* have perceived whatever it was only indirectly—e.g. because it was difficult to see the procession over the heads of the crowd. Here again, our meaning would need to be made clear.

But now, none of this applies, apparently, to the philosopher's use of these words. For it is not that there are special cases in some way unlike normal cases of perceiving something, though sufficiently similar to be described as cases of 'indirect perception'.

[1] Op. cit. p. 18.

For the fact seems to be that anything, or practically anything, which would ordinarily be said to be perceived *at all* is said by the philosopher to be perceived 'indirectly', and the only things he allows to be directly perceived is a class of entities simply not figuring in our ordinary discourse.

Not merely should we reserve the expression 'indirect perception' for special, abnormal cases. 'If', Austin says, 'we are to be seriously inclined to speak of something as being perceived indirectly, it seems that it has to be the kind of thing which we (sometimes at least) just perceive, or could perceive, or which—like the backs of our own heads—others could perceive. For otherwise we don't want to say that we perceive the thing *at all*, even indirectly.'[1] But, in the philosopher's use, 'it seems that what we are to be said to perceive indirectly is *never*—is not the kind of thing which ever *could* be—perceived directly'.

As to what the philosopher's use is, Austin professes himself to be quite unclear. It is thus not at all easy for him to assess the validity of the 'argument from illusion', since he is unclear what it is supposed to establish. He does, however, undertake a detailed examination of this argument, and reaches the conclusion that it proves nothing whatever of any significance. Disposing of the argument is a matter, he says, 'of unpicking, one by one, a mass of seductive (mainly verbal) fallacies, of exposing a wide variety of concealed motives'.[2] I shall not enter into all the subtlety and detail with which he does this. I shall state as briefly as possible with what steps of the argument he finds fault and for what reasons.

To begin with, Austin does not deny that things may sometimes, in an obvious sense, look, feel, etc. other than they are. He does not, for example, deny that a straight stick part of which is in water looks bent. But why, he asks, does this constitute any objection to saying that we *see* the stick, or even that we see it 'directly'? Why may we not say that what we see is a *straight stick partly submerged in water* which, as the natural result of this, looks bent? And whatever reason is there for supposing that there must necessarily be something *else*, other than the stick and the water, which we also see—something, that is, which really is bent. Similarly

[1] Op. cit. p. 18.   [2] Op. cit. pp. 4–5.

'if, to take a rather different case, a church were cunningly camou-
flaged so that it looked like a barn, how could any serious question be raised about what we see when we look at it? We see, of
course, *a church* that now *looks like a barn*. We do *not* see an
immaterial barn, an immaterial church, or an immaterial anything
else. And what in this case could seriously tempt us to say that we
do?'[1] And any other example could be dealt with in the same
manner. Why, for us to be able to say that a thing is seen (even
'directly'), does it *have* to look in all respects as it is? And why,
if in some respects a thing looks other than it is, must something
else also be seen, something fundamentally different in kind from
the thing in question? If a thing *looks* X but is not really X, why
does this license the conclusion that there is anything seen which
is X?

But how about cases of complete hallucination where, as Austin
agrees, 'something totally unreal is *conjured up*'? Here, he has to
admit, we cannot be said to *perceive* whatever it is that we seem
to perceive. He is evidently prepared to admit also that we do
perceive, or at any rate experience, something. The example he
chooses to discuss is that of the mirage, of which, however, he
says that though we may want some name for the thing we experience, 'the fact is that it already has a name—a *mirage*'.[2] Why,
therefore, call it a 'sense-datum'? One might, indeed, raise the
question, which Austin does not himself raise, whether there is
always a name so conveniently ready to hand to deal in like manner with other cases of hallucination. But doubtless we could,
failing anything else, always say that we experienced 'a hallucination of' whatever it might be. So we could always, it seems, do
without 'sense-data'.

And thus we pass to the next stage in the argument, the stage
where it is alleged that there is no difference in kind between those
experiences which we have when what we are perceiving looks,
or otherwise appears, in all respects as it is and those we have when
it appears other than it is, or when we are not (really) perceiving
it at all. But how far, Austin asks, is this actually true? He proceeds
to cite a number of cases which he thinks demonstrate that it is

[1] Op. cit. p. 30.   [2] Op. cit. p. 32.

not universally true. Could it, he asks, 'be seriously suggested'[1] that in dreaming we are being presented to the Pope, we undergo experiences identical in kind with those we should undergo if we really were presented to him? 'Again, it is simply not true to say that seeing a bright green after-image against a white wall is exactly like seeing a bright green patch actually on the wall; or that seeing a white wall through blue spectacles is exactly like seeing a blue wall; or that seeing pink rats in D.T.s is exactly like really seeing pink rats; or . . . that seeing a stick refracted in water is exactly like seeing a bent stick.'[2] He is prepared to admit that there may be some cases in which experiences of these two contrasted kinds really are exactly alike, but this does not, he insists, apply to anything like all cases of this sort.

But does the fact that it may apply to some 'require us to drag in, or even to let in, sense-data? No. For even if we were to make the prior admission (which we have so far found no reason to make) that in the "abnormal" cases we perceive sense-data, we should not be obliged to extend this admission to the "normal" cases too. For why on earth should it *not* be the case that, in some few instances, perceiving one sort of thing is exactly like perceiving another?'[3] What is wrong, for example, with the idea that seeing the reflection of a thing in a mirror might sometimes be exactly like seeing the thing itself or that seeing a lemon might sometimes be exactly like seeing a bar of soap?

With that I conclude my summary of Austin's objections to the argument from illusion. They do show, at the very least, that were one to remain convinced that the argument, or something like it, could be put to some profitable use, then it would have to be stated with very much greater care and probably at very much greater length.

I do not, however, believe that we can let the matter rest at that. Austin has not, in my opinion, succeeded in disposing of the problem of perception;[4] and I intend now to give my reasons for thinking this. I do not want to revive the argument from illusion, as cast in its present form; but I *shall* try to rehabilitate the sense-datum/physical-object dichotomy, or at any rate one version of it,

---

[1] Op. cit. p. 48.   [2] Op. cit. p. 49.   [3] Op. cit. p. 52.   [4] See above, p. 17.

and I shall advance in its favour some of the considerations, and others arising from them, that are deployed by the argument from illusion. But first, I should like to quote a highly pertinent remark made by Professor P. F. Strawson in a broadcast he delivered not long ago on Austin's work. Even, he said, when the traditional route to the problem of perception via the argument from illusion has been blocked, 'there is no reason to think that nothing in the least like the underlying traditional dichotomy can be salvaged in any form. It might be salvaged in the form, say, of a distinction between public objects of perception on the one hand and private perceptual experiences on the other'.

This is, more or less, the form in which I shall undertake to salvage it. I shall avoid, however, making use of those notoriously slippery words 'public' and 'private'. I shall express the distinction I favour simply as that between, on the one hand, the things in our physical environment which we perceive and on the other, the experiences which we have *when* we perceive them.

The first member of this pair seems quite unexceptionable. We shall eventually examine in detail the various properties serving to characterize these things. But for the time being, 'the things in our physical environment which we perceive' seems an altogether innocuous phrase, offering no possible ground for a charge of obscurity or tendentiousness, even if the precise nature of these things is as yet undecided.

The other half of this dichotomy, the experiences which we have when we perceive things, is not, I fear, quite such plain sailing. What about this word 'experience'? Well, first of all, how far and in what sorts of ways do or might 'perceptual experiences' figure in our ordinary, everyday conversation? I am well aware that I lack the linguistically keen ears of an Austin, but it seems that I must face this question if I am to evade the charge of erecting a false dichotomy on yet another surreptitious misuse of language. Here, then, are some things that anyone might, at certain times, reasonably and properly say.

'Yesterday I had the exciting experience of seeing the Prime Minister walk out of 10 Downing Street.'

24

'Seeing Aunt Cynthia after all these years, looking so old and haggard, was a terrible experience.'

'People who suffer from D.T.s sometimes have the experience of seeing pink rats.'

'I don't know how to describe the experience I had when I first came round from the anaesthetic. Nothing looked in the least normal.'

(These and most of the further examples that I shall give later of 'perceptual experiences' are taken from the sense of sight. I think that if I succeed in establishing the validity of my dichotomy for this sense, then it can be seen to be valid *a fortiori* for the other senses also. It is in the realm of sight that it is most hard to swallow. It is true that since 'illusions' of touch are much less common than 'illusions' of sight,[1] we can place greater reliance on the information about things that we obtain by touching them; and this has led some philosophers to regard the sense of touch as affording us a uniquely 'direct' awareness of physical objects. But the fact remains that, for reasons which I shall give,[2] it would probably be fairly easy to persuade almost anyone of moderate intelligence that an object we touch and the sensation of touch which it induces in us are two separate things. In any case, as I shall argue later, and as seems indeed fairly obvious, the sense of sight is, for us who possess it, by far the most important in supplying us with knowledge of our physical environment. Hence it is with visual perception that I shall be most preoccupied.)

To consider now these examples, do they show that it would be correct to speak of having an 'experience' *whenever* we see something, no matter what it is? Well, in practice, it seems that we generally[3] reserve the word for cases which in one way or another are unusual, out-of-the-ordinary, whether unusually exciting, like seeing the Prime Minister, unusually terrible, like seeing

---

[1] Though not, as we shall see, entirely non-existent.

[2] See Section IV, pp. 99–100.

[3] Though not always, as I shall point out presently.

Aunt Cynthia, or just in themselves unusual, like 'seeing' pink rats or seeing things in an abnormal way under the influence of an anaesthetic. If I were to ask someone whether he had had the experience of seeing his toothbrush that morning, I should expect some such reply as: 'I cleaned my teeth as usual, so of course I saw it; but considering I do so every morning and every night of my life, you could hardly say that it was much of an experience'. If I were to go on and ask if he had ever seen the Prime Minister, he might reply: 'As a matter of fact I did once. Now that was a *real experience*'.

But I think, all the same, that if a philosopher uses the word 'experience' in such a way that in *any* case of seeing (or otherwise perceiving) something, the percipient is to be said to have an experience, no one could rightly accuse him of misusing language. And I would like at this stage to make one very general point, which seems well worth making even if it should not be pressed too far.

Austin has emphasized *ad nauseam* that words and expressions frequently have a large variety of different uses in different cases, and that the precise meaning which any sentence has on any given occasion of utterance depends in part on the context, and in general the complete set of circumstances, in which it is being used. There is, however, one (to us) very important context which, curiously enough, he appears himself to have completely overlooked. That is the context of *philosophical discussion*.

Language, as Austin is at pains to make clear, is an infinitely flexible instrument which can always be adapted, and is constantly having to be adapted, to meet new kinds of situations, or, more generally, to deal with new kinds of things that we want to say. And what is more, such is its scope that when, as happens all the time, we use the same word or expression in slightly different ways in order to express different kinds of things, it is seldom necessary that we should on each separate occasion first go through the laborious business of explaining our use of it on that occasion. For as a rule our use is perfectly plain from the context. Now, there is no reason at all why a person who is talking or writing philosophy should not use *some* words in a slightly different way from that in which he or anyone else would use them in ordinary conversation, yet his use of them be just as plain in its philosophical context as would be the other, non-philosophical uses in *their* appropriate contexts. Austin sometimes gives the impression of thinking that one can take any single remark made by a philosopher, ask oneself 'In what circumstances would it be correct to utter these words in "ordinary" discourse?', and on finding that the answer is Never, conclude that no one who paid due attention to the correct use of words would ever contemplate making this remark (unless the philosopher is avowedly using the words in some special, technical sense of his own, which he has first carefully explained). Now of course it may well be that the philosopher's meaning really is obscure, or that what he says really is absurd. And it may be that a consideration of the correct 'ordinary' uses of the relevant words is the best way of bringing oneself to appreciate that this is so. But equally it *may* be that even though his use of certain words does not correspond exactly with any of their 'ordinary' uses, yet his meaning is none the less clear for that.

Now I do think that a sizeable number of the philosophical assertions which are dismissed by Austin on the strength of his linguistic findings are not by any means as clear as one would wish. At the same time, I believe that many of them deserve to be treated with considerably more sympathy than he gives them, and that with care one can find a reasonably natural sense— natural, that is, in a philosophical context—in which some of them are actually true. I shall in due course suggest how, for example, we should construe the assertion that physical objects are never 'directly perceived' (or, as it is sometimes put, to my mind more happily, are never 'directly *experienced*').

The immediate purpose of this digression, however, was to suggest that the word 'experience' (as used in connection with perceiving) is one which quite naturally and automatically takes on a slightly different usage in philosophical discussion from that which it has in our unreflecting everyday talk. Its usage becomes, if you will, more *refined*, but without being in the least strained or artificial. And it should be noted that it is not *only* philosophical contexts to which this applies. A psychologist might, of course, regularly use the word in ways similar to those in which a philosopher uses them. But so might the humblest of laymen who was given to speculation about 'the workings of the mind'. 'It's amazing to think what a complex animal we must be even to be able to have so familiar and humdrum an experience as that of seeing a toothbrush.' Not, one may think, a very profound remark; but both the clarity and the correctness of its expression are wholly beyond reproach. And it affords an exception to the point made above that it is generally only out-of-the-ordinary cases of seeing something which warrant the use of the word 'experience'.

Suppose, again, that someone who suffered from D.T.s was describing one of his spells of hallucinations. He might say: 'As I walked up the garden path, I was accompanied at first by a pink rat. After this had gone on for a few seconds, my experience became completely normal again'.

The word 'experience' is here being used in a slightly different manner from that in which we should say that seeing the Prime Minister was, whereas seeing our toothbrush was not, a 'real experience'. And we must allow that it is being put to one of its (relatively) less common uses as the result of the unusual nature of the subject under discussion—the hallucinations of a D.T.s sufferer. But what we are not obliged to say is (a) that what is being said is in the least bit obscure, (b) that the English is in any respect whatever imperfect, or even (c) that in order to deal with the special, unusual subject-matter, the ordinary usage of the word 'experience' has had to be stretched—still less, of course, that it is being used in a technical sense. It is indeed the case, as Austin points out, that it is sometimes either necessary or convenient to stretch the ordinary usage of words in order to 'accommodate exceptional situations'.[1] And this does apply here to the words 'accompanied by a pink rat'. For of course he was not really accompanied by a pink rat. He did not even really *see* a pink rat— for there was no pink rat there to be seen, though again he might say that he did without being misunderstood. On the other hand, it really *was* the case that after it had seemed for a few seconds as though he were seeing a pink rat *his experience became completely normal again*.

[1] Vide *Sense and Sensibilia*, pp. 90-1.

It is only to be expected that when the subject under discussion is out-of-the-ordinary, not the sort of subject people often discuss, and therefore one wants to express unusual sorts of things, words will automatically get used in various more or less uncommon ways. And one of the chief features of a well-developed language is that this can occur, more often than not, without any feeling of linguistic strain. The description of a person's hallucinations is precisely a case in point. And so equally is the discussion of a philosophical problem. And the word 'experience' is just such a word as is likely, in either of these cases, to undergo a (slight but significant) alteration in its usage.[1]

This is not to imply that we can always find just the right words to convey anything whatever that we may want to say. Thus sometimes, as I have mentioned, strain on language *is* either inevitable or conducive to succinctness, as when the sufferer from D.T.s says that he 'sees' pink rats. Sometimes, again, it may be necessary or convenient to introduce a technical term, or to use an ordinary word in a technical sense, in which case its use needs, for obvious reasons, to be carefully explained. Yet a third possibility is that an ordinary word may be used in a manner that is entirely appropriate *for the particular context*, and which could not conceivably be described as technical, and yet, to avoid any possible risk of misunderstanding or confusion, one takes the precaution of first explaining in what sense one is using the word. I hope myself to make it clear how I propose to use the word 'experience', but I would claim, none the less, that my usage is a completely natural, non-technical one.

[1] Compare in this connection the word 'appear'. Austin points out that if we say of a certain object that it 'appears' to have a certain property, say a certain size, we ordinarily mean by this not that it looks or feels that size, but that it appears to *be* that size. Thus, to take his own example (*Sense and Sensibilia*, pp. 93–4), although a star admittedly looks tiny, we should nevertheless not say that it 'appears tiny' since we should take this to mean, 'To judge from appearances' (Austin's words) it *is* tiny, which is untrue just because everyone knows that any very distant object always looks immeasurably smaller than it is. However, this notwithstanding, the *philosopher* frequently finds it useful, as most of us seldom do, to have some generic verb to cover either the way an object looks *or* the way it feels, sounds, smells or tastes; and for this purpose he speaks in general terms of the ways in which objects (perceptually) *appear* to us. And no one could conceivably accuse him of thereby misusing language.

It might be wondered why I am so insistent on making this claim. After all, it may be said, if I do succeed in making my usage clear, then what does it matter whether it ought properly to be called a technical usage or not? Unfortunately, however, making clear one's use of a term to everyone's satisfaction is often a very difficult business in philosophy, and whether one has succeeded in doing so is liable to be a matter of earnest dispute. So much, after all, may depend on it (e.g. the answer to the question: Is there a problem of perception?). Any attempt to reinstate the sense-datum/physical-object dichotomy is bound to meet with resistance from some quarters, and the type of resistance that I most anticipate is an appeal to 'ordinary' language to show, first, that my use of 'experience' is thoroughly abnormal and secondly, that only by using a normal word in an abnormal way have I given any appearance of promoting my dichotomy. It is in any case fashionable in contemporary philosophy to regard suspiciously any tampering with the uses of words for whatever purpose as being all too likely to result in confusion and distortion. I have tried to forestall suspicion of this sort by urging that I intend to indulge in no such tampering. Moreover, one of the ways in which I propose to explain my use of this word is to point to certain (admittedly special) non-philosophical contexts in which it might —as it seems to me—be put, quite correctly and properly, to just the use I want.

I shall now proceed with my explanation. We have seen already that this word need not be confined, in its correct usage, to unusual cases of perceiving something. There is nothing illegitimate in our saying that it is impossible to perceive *anything* without undergoing an experience. There is, however, one further respect in which my own intended usage differs from other, more common usages.

I have already had occasion to point out how, as a rule, it enters into the meaning of the word 'see', or any other verb of perception, that what is perceived must really exist. Thus if I am seeing a table, then it follows, by definition, that there is a table which I am seeing. In special cases, it is convenient to stretch the ordinary meaning of the word so that this no longer applies. But even though we may say that a person 'sees' pink rats, we are quite prepared to say also that he cannot really be seeing them since there are none to be seen. Furthermore, though I doubt whether we should say that he cannot really be having the *experience* of seeing them, we certainly might say that the experience he is having cannot really be that of *seeing* them. Really seeing things is the sort of experience he has after 'his experience has become completely normal again'. So it seems as if whether or not one is really seeing things (or otherwise perceiving them) constitutes a difference in the nature of one's experience. I want, however, to use the word 'experience' in such a way that this is not so. Can such a use be defended?

Suppose that someone of a very pedantic and at the same time unimaginative turn of mind professes to be unclear what is meant by having a hallucination. Unable to understand how it is possible to 'see things that aren't there', he seeks enlightenment from one who claims to have been the victim of a particularly vivid hallucination. Let us suppose that he was once (really) attacked by a bull and that this left such a traumatic mark on him that when, on a subsequent occasion, he was rash enough to enter the field in which it happened, he 'saw' a hallucinatory bull charging at him, looking exactly like, and just as real as, the previous one—with the result that for a moment he thought it really was the same animal. He is now submitted to the following interrogation about this incident.

'To begin with, did you or did you not, on that second occasion, see a bull?'

'Well, no, I didn't really *see* a bull, because, as I presently realized, no bull was in fact there. But it seemed exactly *as if* I were seeing one.'

'All right. But would you explain to me what precisely you mean when you say "it seemed exactly as if" you were seeing what in fact you were not seeing. What confuses me are these words "seemed as if". Are you saying that while no seeing-of-a-bull occurred, something *else* exactly like seeing a bull did take place? If so, what was this something else and in what respects was it exactly like seeing a bull, since clearly if it was not seeing a bull it cannot have been exactly like it in all respects?'

'Yes, that is more or less right. This incident was not, certainly, identical in all respects with the one that occurred previously. Whereas before there was a bull a short distance in front of my body, charging at me, this time there was no bull anywhere near my body (which was why I didn't *see* a bull). But this—the presence in the one case, the absence in the other, of a bull in the vicinity of my body—was the only respect in which the two incidents differed from one another. As regards the actual *mental experiences* that I had on the two occasions—as distinct from my physical environment—these, nearly enough anyway, were identical. What I meant in saying that it seemed exactly as if I were seeing a bull was that, although no bull was there, nevertheless the *experience* I was having was exactly the sort one would expect to have if one really were seeing a bull.'

Unless his interrogator were not merely pedantic and unimaginative, but stupid as well, then the only possible comment he could now make would be that the matter had been made admirably clear. Even for one who understands what is meant by having a hallucination, the word 'experience', whose meaning in this context is both natural and obvious, makes it possible to provide an illuminating analysis of this concept, while at the same time bringing to light a distinction of great philosophical importance.

Now it does seem to me that some of the facts brought to our notice by the argument from illusion do serve to strengthen our willingness to accept this distinction. The way in which they do so is by bringing home to us the fact that, for any single perceptual experience which we have at any time, it would be possible, logically, for us to have exactly the same experience, yet for even our immediate physical environment to be entirely different from what it in fact is.

The case of complete hallucination is in some ways the most useful example, even though it has the drawback of being relatively unfamiliar. The undisputed fact of which we are bidden to take note is that sometimes hallucinations do occur. For example, people see mirages. Now, according to the argument from illusion, what a person is directly perceiving—or directly *experiencing* (to use a term that is far preferable)—when he is seeing a mirage is similar in kind to what he would be directly experiencing if he were seeing a real oasis. And this is perfectly correct if what we take it to mean is that the actual experience he is having is of a kind similar to the one he would be having if he were seeing a real oasis. It is just because it *is* of a similar kind that he is seeing a hallucinatory oasis.

There is no reason why it should necessarily be of exactly the same kind. No doubt there is as a rule some difference between a hallucinatory experience and that occasioned by our really seeing the thing in question. For example, a hallucinatory object may look fuzzy; or, even if we are taken in at the time, we may afterwards decide that in some way it did not quite have the look that a real object of the same sort would have had. And if we are not taken in, then this in itself will give rise to a further abnormality in the character of our experience.

But all this is really beside the point. For even if Austin is right, as he very well may be, in insisting that seeing a mirage is unlikely to be exactly like seeing a real oasis, what matters is that it is possible, i.e. logically possible, that it should be. It is possible that a person should have *exactly* the same experience as he would expect to have if he saw a real oasis, yet no oasis be there. Nor, of course, is it only oases to which this applies, for it applies to any item whatever in our physical environment that we care to choose. And the simple reason why it applies is that our perceptual experiences are something quite separate and distinct from the things in our physical environment which we do or could perceive. This would be so even had nobody ever in fact been hallucinated. But were we not able to point to actual cases of hallucination, then we might well fail to recognize its truth. As it is, even if seeing a mirage is not exactly like seeing a real oasis, it is going to be very hard for anyone to deny that it could be. Things would only need to be a little bit different from what they are. Perhaps some hallucinations *are* exactly like seeing the real thing; but even if this is never the case we have no difficulty in understanding the suggestion that it might be. And what would it be for seeing a mirage to be exactly like seeing a real oasis? Answer: Despite the presence in the latter case, the absence in the former of an oasis in a certain region of our environment, the actual *experiences* that we should have in the two cases would be of precisely the same kind.

The examples of cases in which something that we are really seeing looks other than it is point, though in a slightly different way, to the same conclusion—the necessity to distinguish in a hard-and-fast manner between perceptual experiences and environmental objects of perception. Consider the straight stick which looks bent when partly immersed in water. In the first place, we must agree with Austin that it does not look *exactly* like a bent stick not in water. Because, quite apart from anything else, we can see the water as well as the stick. We cannot, therefore, for this as well as for other reasons, say, roundly, that the experience a person has when he sees a straight stick in water is identical in kind with that which he has when he sees a bent stick out of water. But even so, the experiences which he has in the two cases do resemble one another in certain important respects—they resemble one another to an extent at least which makes it true to say that in both cases the stick 'looks bent'.

Now what, one might ask, could possibly be found so significant in the fact that two things of different shapes may sometimes look the same shape? As Austin says, 'Does anyone suppose that if something is straight, then it jolly well has to *look* straight at all times and in all circumstances?'[1] No of course, we know only too well that it is possible for things to look other than they are. And what assures us beyond any doubt that they *can* do so is the fact that sometimes they do. But once assured of this possibility, it then becomes exceedingly difficult to see how we can impose any definite limit to the amount a thing could, logically, differ in the way it looks from the way it is. Even if, in practice, a thing that looks like something else does not as a rule look exactly like it (e.g. a straight stick like a bent stick), still the suggestion that it might makes perfectly good sense. It is not nonsense to suppose that there might be a type of glass worn, we may suppose, in the

[1] *Sense and Sensibilia*, p. 29.

manner of a contact lens through which a straight stick—on dry land—looked exactly as a bent stick would look if viewed with the naked eye.

But at least it would still look like a stick. However, in the first place, it is of course possible even in real life for a thing of one sort to look like, and perhaps be mistaken for, a thing of a quite different sort. But further; one can imagine a lens which distorted the shapes, sizes and colours of things out of all recognition, so that, for example, the dining-room table seen through it, however closely, looked exactly like a frog seen with the naked eye. Perhaps there would come a point when the way a thing looked differed so much from the way it was that we should hesitate to say we were seeing it any longer. But this does not matter to the argument. In any case, the point chosen would necessarily be a completely arbitrary one.

If, now, we are prepared to say—and there is no hard-and-fast rule to stop us—that we *should* be seeing whatever was 'there', no matter how much the lens were to distort its appearance,[1] then we may say that anything could, given the right kind of lens, be made to look exactly like anything else. If, as is obviously possible, someone were to wear one of these lenses without knowing it or without being aware of its distorting effects, and consequently be actually taken in by the deceptive appearances of what he saw through it, then the experience that he would have when seeing the dining-room table through it might be identical *in all respects* with that which he would have if he saw a frog with the naked eye.

The conclusion I want to draw from this fanciful story is this. Given any single case in which I am seeing some object in my environment, it would be logically possible for me to have exactly the same experience, and yet be seeing something completely different, which looked exactly like the thing that I thought I was seeing. Here, then, is a further consideration which compels us,

---

[1] In order to single out the particular thing which corresponded with any particular appearance, in order, for example, to know that what looked like a frog was the dining-room table and not the adjoining chair, we might need to know in just what systematic ways the lens carried out its distorting effects.

surely, to acknowledge the distinction between two quite separate things—the experience that I have, and the thing in my environment that I see.

In fact, we can detect shades of this distinction enshrined in Austin's own words, if we examine them carefully enough. 'It is simply not true', he remarks, 'that seeing a bright green after-image against a white wall is exactly like seeing a bright green patch actually on the wall; or that seeing a white wall through blue spectacles is exactly like seeing a blue wall; or that seeing pink rats in D.T.s is exactly like really seeing pink rats;' and so on. Now in one sense each of these cases is indeed different from the other, inasmuch, simply, as an after-image is a different sort of thing from a patch actually on a wall, or a white wall is from a blue one, or a hallucinatory rat is from a real one. Is it for this reason, then, that Austin says that seeing one member of each pair is not exactly like seeing the other? No, this is certainly *not* his reason, for a bit later he declares himself anxious not to deny that sometimes perceiving two different sorts of things *may* be exactly alike. 'Why on earth', he asks, 'should it *not* be the case that, in some few instances, perceiving one sort of thing is exactly like perceiving another?' So, he evidently recognizes a distinction between, on the one hand, what it is that we perceive and on the other, 'what it is like' to perceive it. 'What it is like' to perceive two different sorts of things may (sometimes) be exactly the same. (And surely even in the cases where he says it is not, it *could be*.) But what is meant here by speaking of 'what it is like' to perceive something? The answer is that it is to speak, in a conversational manner, of the actual experience that a person has when he perceives it.

Incidentally, even the word 'experience', *used in just this sense*, creeps into Austin's lines, sometimes, it is true, in inverted commas, but not always. For example, in answer to the question whether dreaming I am being presented to the Pope is exactly like actually being presented to him, he replies: 'Quite obviously not. After all, we have the phrase "a dream-like quality"; some waking experiences are said to have this dream-like quality. . . . If dreams were not "qualitatively" different from waking experiences, then *every* waking experience would be like a dream.'[1] Now there is, of course, a sense in which there is all the difference in the world between dreaming I am being presented to the Pope and actually being presented. For the fact that in the former case I am not (really) being presented, whereas in the latter case I am, constitutes a vast difference. But it is not *this* difference to which Austin is referring. What he is referring to—this time quite explicitly—is the difference in quality (even) of the actual *experiences* that I should have in the two cases. In the one case their quality would be dream-like, in the other it almost certainly would not be. If even Austin uses the word 'experience' in this sense— the sense in which *some* waking experiences are very like dream experiences—then we can be quite sure that it is a legitimate sense, one that is sanctioned even by the conventions of 'ordinary' language.

The part of the argument from illusion which states that there is no difference in kind between the experiences we have when what we are seeing looks as it is and those we have when it looks other than it is or when we are not seeing it at all needs, I agree, to be qualified. But it contains, none the less, an important element of truth. For the fact is that whether what we are seeing really is as it looks, and whether we are really seeing it, depends, not on the character of our experience, but on the character of our immediate physical environment. Given any case in which something in fact is as it looks, it would be possible, logically, for it to be other than it looked, or even not be there at all, and yet for us to have exactly the same experience.

This, I contend, is the justification for saying that things in our physical environment are never, and never could be, 'directly perceived' or (better) 'directly experienced'. What this amounts to is that no such thing can ever *become part of our experience*. No matter what the environmental 'object of perception' may be, it must necessarily be something totally separate and distinct from any perceptual experience. There is no possible perceptual experience whose existence would logically guarantee *its* existence.

This is indeed, long as I have been in seeking to establish it,

[1] *Sense and Sensibilia*, pp. 48–9.

nothing more than a truism. The word 'experience', in this particular sense, is being used to *denote* something separate and distinct from that which is denoted by the words 'environmental object of perception'. Their separateness and distinctness become apparent, inevitably, only after we have properly understood just what this sense of 'experience' is. The argument from illusion may be useful in that it may help us to do this.

The difficulties of construing this word are not, as a matter of fact, the only obstacle in the way of our accepting this distinction. There is also a psychological reason why we may find ourselves resisting this 'cutting off' from our experience of the physical world. Of this I shall say something in the following section.[1]

I have so far made no specific mention of the sense of touch. However, the distinction between perceptual experiences and environmental objects of perception applies just as much here as it does in the realm of sight. That is to say, the experience that I have when I touch something and the thing that I touch are two quite different things. No matter what the thing may be, it is logically possible that I should touch something totally different or not touch anything at all, yet have just the same experience. That tactual hallucinations are possible cannot be disputed because, like visual ones, they sometimes actually occur. It has been pointed out by Professor Price[2] that, for example, 'a man whose leg has been amputated feels pressure upon his now non-existent foot' or that 'when my hat is taken off my head, I still continue to feel it there for a time'. He mentions also that it is possible to stimulate the brain of a conscious person with an electric current in such a way that he feels as if someone were stroking his finger. It is no use, therefore, trying to maintain—as some philosophers actually have maintained—that the sense of touch, if not the sense of sight, really does give us 'direct access' to the physical world.

The dichotomy which I have been urging, thus stated as that between perceptual experiences and environmental objects of perception, seems to give rise to precisely the same problems as it was

---

[1] P. 51.   [2] H. H. Price, *Perception* (Methuen, 1932), pp. 29–30.

thought to do when described as that between direct and indirect objects of perception. Let us see first how these problems would be stated in detail by the use of this latter terminology, and then translate into our own.

The things that make up our physical environment are never directly perceived. Even if, therefore, we can give some sense to saying that they are perceived indirectly, how can we ever know that at any time we really are perceiving in this way what we think we are perceiving? No matter what it is that we are *directly* perceiving, the fact that we *are* so perceiving it seems logically compatible with the fact that we may *not* be perceiving, even indirectly, either this particular physical object or even any at all. How, therefore, are our beliefs about the physical world to be justified? And moreover, what is it to perceive a physical object? In what way(s) must it be related to the thing we perceive directly? Perhaps by answering *this* question, we shall have paved the way for an answer to the first question.

One drawback to this formulation of the problems is that while there is, as I have tried to show, a sense in which it is true that things in our environment are never directly perceived, no sense has yet been given to saying that something else *is*. It is this question that will be discussed in the next section. However, it is possible to restate these problems in the terms that I have advocated without having to bring in 'immediate objects of perception'. This I shall now do.

Even if it is supposed that things in our physical environment are sometimes perceived, they are necessarily something completely separate and distinct from the actual experiences that we have when we perceive them. How, therefore, can we ever know that at any time we really are perceiving what we think we are perceiving? No matter what experience we are having, our having it affords no logical guarantee that any particular item in the environment, or even any at all, is being perceived by us. It seems, at any rate, that it would be possible, logically, for us to have had throughout the entire course of our lives precisely the experiences that we have had, yet for even our immediate physical environment to have been throughout totally different from what it in fact was. Perhaps there might even not have been a physical world. There seems, therefore, no contradiction involved in the suggestion that we might have had just the experiences we have had, yet never at any time have been perceiving what we thought we were perceiving. So again, we find ourselves asking: How are our beliefs about the physical world to be justified? And again we may want to know what is involved in perceiving a physical object. In what way(s) must something in the environment be related to someone's experience if we are to say that it is being perceived? To echo the title of this book, how is contact established with the physical world?

This formulation of the problems can hardly be felt to make them appear any less formidable than the original one did. It may yet turn out that the 'problem of perception' is, in some sense, an unreal problem, one that dogs us only as a result of insidious fallacies in our thinking. But at least this would have to be shown. The task would still remain, not exactly of solving this problem, but of pinpointing those misconceptions and false assumptions that have given rise to it. I have tried in this first section to rule out one possible way of disposing of it, namely by attempting à la Austin to invalidate the setting up in the first place of that dichotomy without which the problem cannot be stated.

II

SENSE-DATA

I claim so far to have established the validity of a sharp dichotomy between (a) the things in our physical environment which we perceive and (b) the experiences which we have when we perceive them. This dichotomy provides us with a sense in which we can vindicate the view that physical objects are never 'directly perceived' or 'directly experienced'. But those philosophers who have held this view have generally held also that in perception we do directly perceive or experience something; and they have called this thing a 'sense-datum'. What sense can we attach to this further doctrine?

Well, to say that in perception we directly experience something, though not the thing in our environment which we perceive, may be taken to mean no more than that in perception there is some experience which we have, even though this is something entirely distinct from the thing in our environment which we perceive. And this, if my arguments have been sound, is certainly true. But if no more is implied than this, then it is not immediately clear what use there is for the term 'sense-datum', what it is supposed to serve as the name of. The distinction between perceptual experiences and environmental objects of perception has no tendency to suggest that whenever we perceive something in our environment, there must always be something *else* (for which we want a name) which we also perceive in at all the same sense of 'perceive' (except 'directly' instead of 'indirectly'). And I am in fact anxious to avoid making any such suggestion. If I am seeing, say, a table, then we are able to distinguish between (a) the thing that I am seeing—i.e. the table and (b) the experience that I am having. But nothing is achieved whatever by introducing a further item into the situation, viz. (c) something other than the table that I am also seeing.

I still believe, however, that there is a legitimate use for the term 'sense-datum'. It has a use in enabling us to describe, in a manner that is convenient for our purposes, the character of our perceptual experiences.

Since one of the tasks we have set ourselves is that of specifying how the things in our environment which we perceive are related to our perceptual experiences, we shall naturally want some means of describing our experiences independently of the things we perceive. Such an independent description is not, for reasons already noted, afforded by such a statement as 'I am now seeing a table'. For we observed that it is part of the meaning of the word 'see'— or any other verb of perception—that what is perceived must really exist: the D.T.s sufferer does not really *see* pink rats just because there are none to be seen. In saying, therefore, that I am seeing a table, I am not *merely* describing my present experience. I am, in addition, affirming that there is a table which I am seeing. How, therefore, is this feature of my statement to be eliminated?

Mr Warnock has suggested that rather than say 'I am now seeing a table', we should say instead '*It seems to me now as if* I were seeing a table'.[1] This statement, it may be thought, is made true solely by my having a particular sort of experience; its truth is unaffected by whether or not there is actually a table (or indeed anything) that I am seeing. An objection that has been raised to such a formula is that we should expect it to be used only by one who was not sure that he really was seeing a table (or who knew he was not) and was hence disposed to employ this non-committal form of words. We should consider it odd for someone to utter these words who had no doubt whatever that he was seeing a table. But the fact that their use would in such a case be inappropriate is not to say they would necessarily express something that was actually false. While they would naturally mislead the person to whom they were addressed into assuming that he *was* in doubt—after all, what would be the *point* of saying 'It seems to me as if I were seeing a table' if he were in a position to say simply 'I

---

[1] G. J. Warnock, *Berkeley* (Penguin Books, 1953), ch. 9.
Warnock's avowed motive for advocating this form of words is a slightly different one from that which I am now mooting, but it amounts in effect to the same thing.

see a table'?—it does not follow that his being in doubt would be part of their meaning, part of what they would actually assert, and not merely imply. It may be urged *against* this that even though the use of these particular words would be peculiar in these circumstances, it would nevertheless be quite natural for someone else to say 'It seems to *him* as if *he* were seeing a table', or for him himself to say on a subsequent occasion 'It *seemed* to me as if I were seeing a table'. These words would indeed imply—though only imply—doubt on this other person's part, or on his own part on this subsequent occasion, as to whether he did see a table (or else certainty that he did not). But they would not imply that he was himself in any doubt at all at the time of having the perceptual experience in question.

It may well be, therefore, that a sentence of the form 'It seems to me now as if I were seeing [or otherwise perceiving] . . .' would indeed serve as a correct description of an ordinary perceptual experience. While admittedly its use for this purpose would in ordinary contexts be pointless and misleading, the same would not apply in our philosophical context, where we have a special reason for wanting to make statements that are descriptive *solely* of our perceptual experiences.

It might, all the same, be objected that these words are so strongly associated with their role in the type of case I have indicated that the use now proposed for them could never lose a certain artificiality. However, the main fault I have to find with this formula is that it fails to make explicit what the peculiar character of any perceptual experience is. To say of someone that it seems to him as if he were seeing a table is just a way of saying that, whether or not he is in fact seeing a table, the situation is exactly like that of seeing a table as far as the actual experience he is having goes—even though it may not be in other respects. He is at any rate having an experience of exactly the sort *one would expect to have if* one were seeing a table. This is the force of the words 'it seems as if'. But then, what sort of an experience *is it* that one has when one sees a table? In a sense, this is something that anyone who has ever seen a table knows. But in philosophizing about perception we want to be able to *state* of what sort this experience is, to have some means of describing its intrinsic character. And it is for this purpose that we have recourse to some such term as 'sense-datum'.

I must now, therefore, undertake to make it clear how I intend to use this term. I shall begin with visual sense-data.

Suppose that I am now looking, from a short distance and in completely normal circumstances, at the top of a square, red book, and am having, therefore, an experience of just the sort that anyone would expect to have who did likewise. We all know, therefore, of exactly what sort this experience is: we all know what, as we say, it is *like* to be looking at a square, red book. Hence there is no question of having to find out what the character of this experience is. The task before us is that of reaching a decision on how best to describe it. Now we remember that I could, logically, have the very same experience, yet neither a book nor anything that looked like a book actually be there. What we have, therefore, to describe is something common both to the ordinary situation where it *would* be there and to the hallucinatory one where it would not.

Well, there is one salient feature present in both the two situations which one might naturally describe, in ordinary words, as *the existence of a square, red colour-patch in my visual field.* It is because of this colour-patch that, in the case where I am not in fact seeing a book, I am said to be having a hallucination of seeing one. It is because of this colour-patch that even though I am not seeing a book, *it seems to me as if* I were. To state that there is this colour-patch in my visual field is to state that I am having a particular sort of experience—and to state nothing more than this. Whether or not there is anything that I am seeing is left entirely unspecified.

It is objected by Austin that there is no warrant for *distinguishing* what I am seeing from what is in my visual field. For, he says, 'coloured shapes, patches of colour, etc. can quite often and correctly be said to *be* the things that we see'.[1] For example, 'it would surely be quite natural and proper to say, "That patch of red there *is* the book" (cf. "That white dot is my house")'.

[1] *Sense and Sensibilia*, p. 136.

I do not deny that we might say these things. But the point is that a statement like 'There is a red patch in my visual field' would be so construed that we should count it as true even if there were nothing whatever 'there' that I was seeing.[1] What it expresses, therefore, is simply the fact that I am having a particular sort of experience. If I am in fact seeing a book, then I could if I chose express this *further* fact by saying 'This red patch is a book'. But it still remains true that to say 'There is a red patch in my visual field' is to make an assertion about something totally different from the book, namely my present experience. And moreover, it is in a *philosophical* context misleading to speak of this colour-patch as 'being' the book, just because it obscures the philosophically, though not otherwise, important distinction between my experience and the thing that I am seeing. Indeed it would in this context be 'quite natural and proper' to say that this patch is *not* the book, but something completely distinct from it.[2] For it is a feature of my experience; whereas the book is not, but is rather an object in my physical environment.

I can, therefore, correctly describe the experience that I have when I look at the square, red book by saying that there is a square, red colour-patch in my visual field. This is a description *merely* of my experience, and would therefore be true even if there were no book there for me to be looking at. Now this colour-patch is an example of a *visual sense-datum*.[3]

[1] No 'stretchings of ordinary words' (Austin's phrase) would be involved if a person were to describe a hallucinatory experience by speaking of certain arrangements of colours in his visual field. It is equally clear that he would not thereby be using words in any uncommon *senses*.

[2] Austin notes (op. cit. p. 98 n.) that even though I could say 'That white dot on the horizon is my house', 'this would not license the conclusion that I live in a white dot'. But why not? Because, surely, the white dot and the house are *really* (regardless of our established ways of talking) two separate things.

[3] Why introduce the technical term 'sense-datum' to denote something for which we already have the perfectly good word 'colour-patch'? The answer is that we want a collective term to denote not only what I may call the 'sensory contents' of our *visual* experiences, to which I am at present limiting my discussion, but the 'sensory contents' of *any* of our perceptual experiences—i.e. whichever of the senses be involved. I shall turn to non-visual sense-data in a moment.

It may be that 'sense-datum' is not the ideal term for the use to which I am putting it, in view of some possible misleading implications of the word

It is in fact convenient, for purely literary reasons, for the word 'sense-datum' to function as the object of some verb which has as its subject a word or phrase denoting the person whose experience is being described. And for this purpose the verb 'experience' seems as suitable as any.[1] The experience now in question is to be described, therefore, by saying that 'I am experiencing a square, red sense-datum'.[2]

I have chosen this particular experience as being one that admits of an unusually simple, straightforward description. As often as not, my visual field is composed of a pattern of colours (or of black and white) possessing extreme variegation. Even in the case just considered, the red patch is presumably not all that there is in my visual field. The question arises, therefore: how many visual sense-data am I to be said at any one moment to be experiencing? And there arises also the further question: for how long is any one such sense-datum to be said to endure through time, before being replaced by another? As an answer to these questions, I cannot do better than to quote from Professor A. J. Ayer's book, *The Problem of Knowledge*.[3]

'At the present moment it seems to me that I see the walls of a house, covered with virginia creeper, and a rose tree climbing to an open window, and two dogs asleep upon a terrace, and a lawn bespeckled with buttercups and clover, and many other things besides. . . . How many visual . . . sense-data am I sensing?[4] And at what point are they replaced by others? If one of the dogs

---

'datum'. Perhaps I should speak instead, as Professor Ayer does in his *Language, Truth and Logic*, of a 'sense-content'. I have decided, however, to retain the more familiar term on account of its prevalence in modern discussions of perception.

[1] It would be perfectly correct English for anyone to speak of 'experiencing coloured shapes'.

[2] I am not suggesting that to describe the contents, at a given moment, of our visual field is to give an *exhaustive* description of our experience at that moment, that there is nothing further to be said about its character. I shall say more about our visual experiences a little further on, and in Section IV I shall undertake to describe them in considerable detail.

[3] Penguin Books, 1956, pp. 109–11. (Macmillan ed. pp. 121–2).

[4] In our terminology, 'experiencing'.

seems to stir in its sleep does this create a new sense-datum for me or merely transform an old one? And if it is to be new, do all the others remain the same? Clearly the answers to these questions will be arbitrary; the appearance of the whole frontage of the house may be treated as one sense-datum, or it may be divided into almost any number. The difficulty is to find a rule that would be generally applicable. It might be suggested, for example, that we should say that there were, for a given observer at any given moment, as many visual sense-data as there were features that he could visually discriminate: but this again raises the question of what is to count as a single feature. And similar objections may be made to any other ruling that I can think of. The correct reply may, therefore, be that these questions do not admit of a definite answer, any more than there is a definite answer to the question how many parts a thing can have, or how much it can change without altering its identity. That is to say, there are no general rules from which the answers to such questions can be derived; but this does not mean that they cannot be given answers in particular cases. In the present instance, I can choose to speak of there being a sense-datum of the rose tree, or a sense-datum of one of its roses, or of one of the petals of the rose. . . . And if it be asked whether my present contemplation of the rose tree yields me one sense-datum of it, or a series, and if it is a series, how many members it has, the answer once again is that there can be as many as I choose to distinguish. No single sense-datum can outlast the experience of which it helps to make up the content; but then it is not clear what is to count as one experience. I can distinguish the experience I am having now from those that I have had at different times in the past, but if I were asked how many experiences I had had, for example, during the last five minutes, I should not know what to answer: I should not know how to set about counting. The question would appear to have no meaning. It does not follow, however, that I cannot at any given moment delimit some experience which I am then having: the boundaries may be fluid, but I can say confidently of certain things that they fall within the experience, and of others that they do not. And for our present purposes this may be all that is required.'

47

To turn briefly to sense-data belonging to the other senses. In the case of touch, the problem is to describe the experience that I have when I touch something, bearing in mind that I could, logically, have the very same experience yet not be touching anything at all. What we have, therefore, to describe is something common both to the ordinary situation where I am touching something and to the hallucinatory one where I am not. Well, what (among other things) is common to them is the fact that in both cases I have a certain *sensation of touch*. And this sensation of touch is a tactual sense-datum.[1] Likewise, the sensations of sound, smell or taste that I have when I hear, smell or taste something are respectively auditory, olfactory and gustatory sense-data.

The view has been widely held that sense-data are purely fictitious entities invented by philosophers on the strength of fallacious arguments such as the argument from illusion. It is true, as Austin has shown,[2] that none of the facts and considerations cited by this argument oblige us in any way to amend or to add to the ordinary common-sense account of what it is that we perceive. And it is true also that philosophers have often, in introducing sense-data, represented themselves as doing just this. It is easy to see, therefore, how they have come to be accused of conjuring up non-existent entities. If, however, it is possible, as I have argued, to salvage the distinction between direct and indirect objects of perception in the form of a distinction between (a) the things in our environment that we perceive and (b) the experiences we have when we perceive them, then it becomes quite easy, in the way I have shown, to reinstate sense-data in a guise that our salvage will allow. We no longer have to say that whenever we perceive something in our environment, there must always be something else of a non-physical nature that we per-

---

[1] Austin himself—unwittingly—notes the existence of 'tactual sense-data'. For he says, in connection with the person who 'feels pressure on his leg' even though it has been amputated: 'The expression "pressure on his leg" can sometimes be used to specify what someone *feels, even if* [i.e. whether or not] his leg has actually been amputated'. (*Sense and Sensibilia*, p. 89. The italics are mine.) By 'what someone feels' he can only mean here: a person's actual sensation of touch.

[2] See Section I, pp. 19–23.

ceive as well. But there is, if my arguments have been sound, one class of things different from anything in our environment which does need to be brought into the picture, namely the experiences we have when we perceive things. And it is simply as a means of describing these that we have introduced the term 'sense-datum'. What were once depicted as objects of perception of a mysterious and suspect kind now reappear as features of our experiences.[1] If once the distinction between environmental objects of perception and perceptual experiences be accepted, and it be properly understood what purpose the term 'sense-datum' is to serve, then it can scarcely any longer be possible to uphold the view that a mythical class of entities has been conjured into existence. For apart from the two members of our dichotomy, no *additional* items have been introduced.

The only question is whether the role that is to be played by the word 'sense-datum' in describing our perceptual experiences can be made sufficiently precise, whether, that is to say, we can find a sufficiently clear sense for descriptions of our experiences in which this word figures. The test of whether we have succeeded in doing this is whether, for any such description, it is clear just what kinds of experiences would count as ones that answered to it. For my part, I see no reason why, in general, this should not be clear. There is no special difficulty in talking about the coloured shapes in our visual field or our sensations of touch, sound, smell or taste. And there can be no objection to our introducing a collective term to cover all of these.

There is, true, one special problem, or rather pair of problems, often raised in connection with sense-data which I should mention in passing, though I shall do no more than this. That is the two related problems of whether it be possible (a) that my sense-data should have characteristics which I fail to notice at the time of experiencing them and (b) that I should be mistaken about the

---

[1] I am not claiming any originality for this view of sense-data. Indeed it will have been noted that Professor Ayer, in the passage quoted above, speaks of a sense-datum as 'helping to make up the content of' a person's experience. My aim in the foregoing pages has been merely to clarify the true nature of sense-data in such a way as to render them immune from the kind of onslaught which Austin and others have made on them.

characteristics of my current sense-data.[1] I do not intend to discuss these questions, since I do not think that answering them would in any way assist us in our discussion of the problems of perception. It might be thought that until they have been answered, the usage of the term 'sense-datum' must remain in some degree imprecise. To this I would reply by drawing attention to the following two points.

First, these two problems are in no way peculiar to sense-data. For they arise to precisely the same extent with *any* items of experience. The question here raised is merely one example of the completely general question: Can our experiences have unnoticed characteristics, and can we be mistaken about the characteristics of our current experiences?[2] If, therefore, we have a problem here over whether any given experience does or does not answer to a given description in terms of sense-data, it is no more of a problem than that arising over the application of *any* sentence describing someone's experience.

Secondly, if there is such a problem, it is *not* a problem about the usage of the word 'sense-datum', about the meaning of sentences in which it figures. For the problem is that, not of knowing what kinds of experiences would answer to any given description in terms of sense-data, but of knowing whether any given experience is or is not of a kind which we know *would* answer to it.

I consider, therefore, that we may proceed without further ado to adopt this term.

We may employ it, as a start, for the purpose of stating in the traditional manner one of the two problems of perception. This is the problem we have so far described as that of specifying how our perceptual experiences are related to the objects in our environment that we perceive. It is obvious that those features of our perceptual experiences which, above all, we want so to relate

[1] By this second question I mean: Is it possible that my current sense-data should *seem* to me to have characteristics which they do not actually have? Clearly it is possible for me to make a verbal error should I undertake to *describe* my sense-data (or indeed anything)—whether to someone else or silently to myself.

[2] Can we, for example, be experiencing pain without noticing that we are, and can we seem to be experiencing pain when really we are not?

are our sense-data. Accordingly, we are now free to state this problem in its familiar terms as that of specifying the relationship between on the one hand our sense-data and on the other the objects in our environment that we perceive.

What needs to be explained, among other things, is the very striking and very puzzling way in which our visual sense-data in particular 'present' to our consciousness those objects that we are said to see. So efficiently do they perform this 'presentative function',[1] such is the 'vividness' of presentation, that it *seems*, undeniably, as though we were somehow involved in a direct 'confrontation' with the physical world—in a way which is very hard to understand in view of the fact that the physical objects we see are something wholly distinct from our visual experiences. Is it not rather *as though* these objects, or at any rate their front surfaces, had actually 'entered into', become a feature of, our experience in a way that is really impossible for them? Is it not, in other words, rather *as though* we were 'directly experiencing' them? This is certainly extremely puzzling; yet it is a plain, indisputable fact about our experience. It is on account of this fact that we hesitate, at first, to accept the view that the objects we see are something quite separate and distinct from our visual experiences. It is on account of this fact too that the problem of justifying our beliefs about the physical world seems at first to be such an unreal one. Had we not reflected on these matters, our instinctive reaction would have been: 'But I can actually *see* this object here with my own two eyes. It is right there in front of me, staring me in the face. What more could be needed to assure me of its existence?' The suggestion that it might not exist—for the reason that no perceptual experience affords any logical guarantee of the existence of any physical object—would have struck us as just plain absurd.

It is not unplausible to suppose that when we are looking, say, at a book, we actually identify the relevant visual sense-datum with the book (or with its front surface):[2] we mistake what is in

---

[1] This expression is borrowed from Professor H. H. Price.

[2] This was the view of Professor H. A. Prichard. Vide *Knowledge and Perception* (Oxford University Press, 1950), ch. 4.

reality a feature of our experience for an item in our physical environment. This would explain why it *seems* as though the book itself were a feature of our experience. I think, however, we may agree with Professor Price[1] that to say this would be to depict ordinary perceptual awareness as a much more intellectual process than it actually is. The question of whether the patch of colour in our visual field is or is not a physical object, or the surface of a physical object, is just not raised at this level.[2] It is raised only in the course of philosophical reflection, and to say otherwise would be to make the ordinary percipient into a philosopher. What *can* be said, again with Professor Price, is that if we do not actually take our visual sense-data to *be* the surfaces of physical objects, at least we are not conscious of them as being anything different. It is left to the philosopher to distinguish them.

We may well agree with Professor Price that this faculty of perceptual awareness, whereby our experience of the physical world is made to seem 'immediate' even though, as we have discovered, it in fact cannot be, 'is surely one of Nature's most ingenious and delicate devices'. And it is not surprising that it has never ceased to present philosophers with the most fascinating of philosophical riddles.

We are faced, then, with the two questions: (i) What is the relationship between sense-data and the physical objects they 'present'? and (ii) How can our beliefs about these objects be justified? Before giving my own answers to these questions, I shall examine, and I hope dispose of, an answer that has frequently been given to them by philosophers in the past.

[1] *Vide* H. H. Price, *Perception*, pp. 143–4.

[2] The fact, noted by Austin and mentioned above (pp. 44–5), that anyone might *say* 'That patch of red is a book' does not contradict this point. For whatever the ordinary person may mean by saying this (and I hope this will become apparent in the course of this book), he cannot be supposed to be *contradicting the philosophical assertion* that the red patch and the book are really two different things. Certainly the ways we have come to talk are likely to embody some rationale, but not necessarily the one which first meets our eye.

III

PHENOMENALISM

The doctrine of *phenomenalism*, by putting forward a certain view of the nature of physical objects, claims both to bring to light the relationship between physical objects and sense-data and to furnish a justification of our beliefs about the physical world. Many philosophers have favoured this doctrine and it still has its adherents at the present day—which is why I am devoting a whole section to it. I shall first expound it in such a way as to make it appear as plausible as possible, and defend it against certain well-known lines of attack which seem to me ineffective. I shall then give my reasons for thinking that it is none the less mistaken.

What it states is that physical objects are nothing *over and above* our perceptual experiences, but are so-called 'logical constructions' out of sense-data. It is by no means entirely obvious what exactly this is supposed to mean, and somewhat differing interpretations have been put on it by different commentators. But I intend to expound it in the only way to which I can myself attach any clear sense.

Let us compare the relationship alleged to obtain between physical objects and sense-data to that which, on any view, does obtain between nations and persons—a comparison that has often been made.

There is a sense in which it would be agreed that a nation is a 'logical construction' out of persons. We may define this sense as follows. Given any true statement about a nation, what *makes* it true is the fact, and only the fact, that particular persons do particular things (at particular times and places) and/or that particular persons *would* do particular things in particular sets of circumstances. Nothing else *in addition* is required in order for such a statement to be true. And, given any true statement affirming the *existence* of a certain nation, what makes this true is the fact, and only the fact, that there exists a certain set of persons between whom certain complex relationships hold—the latter consisting (largely if not entirely) in the fact that certain of these persons act in certain ways *towards*, or would in certain contingencies so act towards, certain others of them; and also, I should add, that various persons in the past as well as the present (e.g. the ancestors of the present monarch) have acted in various ways. To affirm the existence of a 'nation' is not to affirm the existence of a separate— and oddly elusive—entity answering to this name. There is, consequently, a clear sense in which nations are nothing over and above—or as it is sometimes put, are 'reducible to'—persons and their ways of acting. To talk about a nation is always to talk about persons, and not to talk about something with a distinct existence of its own.

Just as a nation can be said to be a 'logical construction' out of persons, so it is maintained by the phenomenalist that a physical object is a 'logical construction' out of sense-data. Given any true statement about a physical object, what (according to him) *makes* it true is the fact, and only the fact, that particular kinds of sense-data are experienced and/or that particular kinds *would* be experienced in particular sets of conditions not actually obtaining. To be more accurate, what the truth of such a statement depends on is the fact that there are or could be experienced particular *series of successive sense-data*—the sorts of series, in fact, that one experiences if one examines a certain object (or set of adjoining objects) bit by bit. No single statement about a physical object requires for its truth anything *besides* the occurrence, or the obtainability, of certain such series of sense-data. To affirm the existence of physical objects is not, therefore, to affirm the existence of a set of objects wholly distinct from, and logically independent of, the totality of sense-data that we do or could experience.

It is important that we should clearly distinguish the phenomenalist's position from certain things which he is emphatically not maintaining, and which have sometimes been attributed to him. He does not hold that there are no such things as physical objects, that any statement which implies their existence is strictly speaking false. His view is, rather, that sense-data (ultimately) constitute the sole *subject-matter* of our ordinary talk about physical objects; or, to reiterate what I have just said, that *facts about* sense-data constitute the sole *truth-conditions* of the statements we make about them. From the fact that speaking of physical objects amounts, in the end, to speaking of sense-data it no more follows that there are no physical objects in the world than it follows, from the fact that speaking of nations amounts to speaking of persons, that there are no nations in the world. Nor does the phenomenalist maintain that physical objects exist only at such times as they are being perceived. He takes a certain view only of what *constitutes* their existing unperceived, the fact, namely, that certain kinds of sense-data *would* be experienced if certain conditions were fulfilled—these conditions being specifiable solely in terms of sense-data.[1] What *can* be attributed to the phenomenalist is the thesis that physical objects are nothing over and above, are not something which exist *in addition to*, the sum of our perceptual experiences[2]—in the same sense as that in which nations are nothing over and above certain sets of persons.

To say that physical objects are 'logical constructions' out of sense-data should not be taken to imply that any statement about a physical object can be *translated*, without a change in meaning, into a statement, or set of statements, mentioning only sense-data. Clearly a statement to the effect, say, that one nation declared war on another cannot be reproduced in a precisely equivalent statement to the effect that certain actions were carried out by certain persons. The reason for this is that there is no one single set of such actions capable of constituting a national declaration of war. And were we to attempt to draw up a list of all those possible sets any *one* of which would constitute it, we should find

---

[1] In other words, the conditions in which each of the relevant sense-data would be experienced are to be specified by stating what other sense-data would need to be experienced first. These consist (roughly) in that sequence of sense-data of which it can be said that anyone who experienced it would, *in fact*, end up with his body so situated as to enable him to perceive a certain physical object. But these sense-data must be defined solely in terms of their intrinsic characteristics. There must be no reference to the position of anyone's body—the latter being itself a physical object and therefore requiring analysis in terms of yet further sense-data.

[2] I shall in due course elaborate on this (p. 61).

this impossible for the reason that such a list would, of necessity, be infinitely long.[1] Exactly the same difficulty would beset us if we undertook to recast any statement about a physical object into a statement, identical in meaning, that referred only to sense-data. No statement about a physical object requires for its truth the occurrence, or the obtainability, of any one specific set of sense-data, but only of one falling within a wide and diffuse range of possible sets. And therefore the most we could do, by way of rendering any such statement in terms of sense-data, would be to list all those possible statements about sense-data of which it could be said that if any *one* of them were true, then the original statement would also be true. But any such list would need, once again, to be infinitely long. In short, we could effect our proposed translation only by putting forward an *infinite disjunction* of statements about sense-data.

But in fact, there is a further reason why our task would be an impossible one. For we could not even specify, in terms of sense-data, any *one* set of circumstances that would ensure the truth of a given statement about a physical object. There is no single statement about sense-data, nor any *finite* set of such statements, that would logically entail any single statement about a physical object. The problem here is that we have always to reckon with the possibility of hallucination, or of lesser illusions. Consider first any one statement to the effect that certain sense-data are or would be experienced in a certain set of conditions. Given that these conditions are themselves specified solely in terms of sense-data, it is consistent with the truth of any such statement that any physical object which is (or would be) taken to be perceived in these conditions either does not exist at all or is not of the kind that it appears to be. For the possibility can never be logically excluded either that any percipient in these conditions is in some way abnormal or that there is some distorting medium between him and the object he is perceiving. And this possibility can never be ruled out no matter how many further statements we may add, so long as we permit ourselves no reference to physi-

[1] I am indebted for this point to Dr D. M. Armstrong. Vide *Perception and the Physical World* (Routledge and Kegan Paul, 1961), pp. 49–50.

cal objects. It could be ruled out only by adding a detailed description of the *physical* conditions in which the relevant sense-data are (or would be) experienced—including the physical state of the person experiencing them. And any attempt to translate such a description into purely sensory terms would meet with the same difficulty all over again. And so we should be compelled to go on adding to our original statement *ad infinitum*.

There is, therefore, no finite set of statements about sense-data the truth of which would constitute either a necessary or a sufficient condition for the truth of any statement about a physical object. But it does not follow from this that physical objects are not 'logical constructions' out of sense-data. I have shown already that it is not possible to state, in terms only of persons and their actions, all of those possible ways whereby one nation may declare war on another. It might perhaps be possible to state any one such way; but in the case of many more logically complex statements about nations—for example, 'Britain is a constitutional monarchy' —I doubt whether we could specify, in these terms, even one set of circumstances logically sufficient for their truth. Their truth would depend largely on the fact that each of a certain set of persons *would* act in a certain way in each of an infinity of possible contingencies—and each such person in a different way in each such contingency. But it still can be said that nations are 'logical constructions' out of persons—in the sense that any statement about a nation depends for its truth solely on a set of facts about persons and their actions, albeit on an infinite, and therefore not fully specifiable, set of such facts. In the same way, it is held that any statement about a physical object depends for its truth solely on a set of facts, infinite in number and likewise unspecifiable, about sense-data.[1]

Finally, given this, what is it to be perceptually aware of a physical object of a particular kind? The answer will have to be that for a person to be said to have such awareness, he must (a) experience a sense-datum or sense-data of a particular kind and (b) (on the strength of this) *take it for granted*, in some sense or

---

[1] If this is not what is meant by saying that physical objects are 'logical constructions' out of sense-data, then I have no idea what *is* meant by it.

other,[1] that infinitely many other ones of particular kinds are obtainable, given the right sets of conditions.

There is no denying that phenomenalism has considerable attraction. In the first place, it would solve the problem of the seeming 'inaccessibility' of the physical world 'behind' our sense-data. It can still be said that we do not 'directly experience' physical objects. A sense-datum is still not literally *part of* a physical object, for to say that physical objects are 'logical constructions' out of sense-data is not to say that they are *composed of* sense-data in the sense in which a wall is composed of bricks. But at any rate, on the phenomenalist view the one is intimately connected with the other. We are not so completely 'cut off from' the physical world as we should seem to be were it something entirely over and above our perceptual experiences.

It might appear, therefore, that only phenomenalism can give a satisfactory account of our 'contact with the physical world'. One might argue that even if there did exist something over and above our experiences, it could in no way concern us. For provided that the course of our experience remained as it is now, it would make no difference to us whether this something did or did not exist. Is it not, therefore, most unplausible to suggest that it is to this that our everyday talk of physical objects refers?

But above all, perhaps, phenomenalism affords us a means of justifying our beliefs about the physical world. For reasons which I have given, no finite number of perceptual experiences can ever provide a logical guarantee of the existence of any physical object. And to this extent it is agreed by the phenomenalist that no statement about a physical object can ever be 'conclusively verified'. But it is claimed that we may have good inductive grounds for believing such a statement to be true.[2] On any occasion when we experience sense-data of any given kind, we may draw on our past experience as a guide to what other sense-data we could also

---

[1] See Section IV, p. 119.

[2] Cf. A. J. Ayer, *The Foundations of Empirical Knowledge* (Macmillan, 1940), pp. 36-46.

experience were we to be placed in the appropriate situations.[1] And by this means we may reasonably assure ourselves that in *any* of an infinite range of possible situations, we should experience such sense-data as need to be obtainable in order for some statement about a physical object to be true. And should we for any reason still not be satisfied, we may put the truth of this statement to any number of further tests. The more of these tests conform in their results with the ordinary course of our past experience, the more likely it becomes that any conceivable other tests we might have made would have done so too. And therefore the greater becomes the inductive probability that the statement being tested is indeed true. Nevertheless, it is to be expected that in most ordinary circumstances we shall be fully justified in relying immediately on the veracity of our senses—even in assuming that some object exists on the basis of a single perceptual experience.

On the other hand, it is urged by those who argue in this way that if physical objects are conceived of as something wholly distinct from all possible experiences, then it is impossible to establish their existence by any valid process of inference. It has been held by some philosophers that their existence can be postulated as the necessary causes of our perceptual experiences. But, as Professor Price has shown at length,[2] the arguments put forward by these philosophers are one and all invalid. Even were we to accept that perceptual experiences must be caused by something 'outside' themselves,[3] this would not enable us (without a host of unwarranted assumptions) to infer the specific nature of any such cause. The conclusion seems, therefore, to be inescapable that by conceiving of physical objects in this fashion, we land ourselves with the absurd result that we can never have the slightest reason for supposing them to exist. Here, then, is one line of thought which

---

[1] It is not suggested that we *consciously recall* our past experience, or that we arrive at our beliefs about physical objects through any conscious process of inference. The phenomenalist is seeking to explain only why these beliefs are, as a matter of fact, well-founded.

[2] H. H. Price, *Perception*, ch. iv.

[3] I should make it clear that the phenomenalist does *not* accept this. He maintains, on the contrary, that the notion of something outside our experience is entirely unintelligible (see Section IV, p. 113 seq.).

any dissenter from phenomenalism must endeavour to demolish. A great many alleged refutations of phenomenalism have been proposed. These have consisted mostly in attempting to show that no analysis is possible in purely sensory terms of this or that universal belief about the character of the physical world. I do not think myself that it can strictly be refuted by any argument of this form. In order to analyze any statement whatever about a physical object, the phenomenalist has only to ask himself how we should *find out* that it is true, what sorts of experiences would lead us to endorse it, since it is in terms of these that his analysis must be effected.[1] And this can never present him with any difficulty of principle. It has been said, for example, that by analyzing physical objects in terms of mere successions of sense-data, and mostly only *possible* ones at that, he has failed to do justice to the fact that a physical object is a solid, unified whole. But he is able to reply to this by showing how its solidity and unity are themselves to be analyzed in terms of certain relations which hold between our successive sense-data.[2] Another charge often imputed to phenomenalism is that it fails to give an adequate account of what it is for an object to exist when no one is perceiving it. It has been said that it gives unperceived objects a merely 'hypothetical' existence in a way that conflicts with our actual conception of them. But the phenomenalist need not accept this. He contends, only, that categorical statements which affirm their unperceived existence are to be *analyzed* in terms of hypothetical statements about *sense-data*. To those who base their objection simply on the fact that he wishes to analyze such statements in terms of *anything* purely hypothetical,[3] he may reply that this precisely begs the question.

[1] By 'analyzing a statement about a physical object' I do not mean: translating it into a set of statements about sense-data, which is impossible, but rather describing in general terms what kinds of sense-data, or sequences of sense-data, would be relevant to the statement's truth (cf. A. J. Ayer, *The Foundations of Empirical Knowledge*, pp. 242–3).

[2] Cf. Ayer, op. cit. pp. 231–2. For a detailed account of the manner in which we are said to 'construct', from our sense-data, the world of physical objects having the properties we ascribe to them, *vide* ibid., Part V, sections 23–4.

[3] Cf. D. M. Armstrong, *Perception and the Physical World*, pp. 53–6. Also Isaiah Berlin, 'Empirical Propositions and Hypothetical Statements', published in *Mind*,

All the same, the phenomenalist's account of the physical world is surely wildly unplausible. The outcome of it is that his combined picture of the universe seems absurdly incomplete.

I have already remarked[1] that physical objects are not, in his view, things that exist over and above the totality of sense-data. It may appear, at first sight, that in saying this I have overlooked all those infinitely numerous sense-data which would exist in certain hypothetical contingencies, and which figure so crucially in the phenomenalist account of what a physical object is. Ought I not, in other words, to say that physical objects are nothing over and above the totality of actual *and hypothetical* sense-data? But this amendment is unnecessary. For a thing that *would* exist is not a thing that *does* exist. If a thing does not actually exist, then it does not exist at all. Hence, whatever the world may be held to contain, one thing it certainly does not contain are 'hypothetical entities'. For it certainly does not contain what does not exist. It contains, therefore, only physical objects and such non-physical entities as there actually are. Nor does the phenomenalist deny that it contains each of these. But in his view, physical objects are not something that exist *in addition to* the totality of perceptual experiences. Therefore the world consists, if he is right, in the sum total of *experience*, and nothing at all else in addition. In short, the mental world is for him the complete world.

Yet surely common sense does not endorse this picture. It thinks of the physical as existing *apart from* the mental, as having a separate existence of its own. Not that this alternative picture is free of drawbacks. For as soon as physical objects are thought of as existing over and above our experiences, they seem to vanish irrevocably 'behind' our sense-data; to become, as it is often put, set apart from us by an 'iron curtain' of sense-data. On the other hand, it is a plain psychological fact that so long as we take into account only the mental constituents of the universe, we feel ourselves to be leaving something out, to be leaving out, in fact, the entire physical world in all its enormity. If our picture is to

1950, and reprinted in *Perceiving, Sensing, and Knowing*, ed. R. J. Swartz (Anchor Books, N.Y., 1965).

[1] P. 55.

seem complete, it is necessary that the earth, the sun, the planets, etc., be introduced as *additional* items. Until they have been so introduced, our universe will seem altogether too sparsely inhabited.

We are faced, therefore, with a dilemma. On the one hand, by rejecting phenomenalism and embracing a 'realist' view of physical objects according to which they are something that exist over and above our perceptual experiences, we seem to make them completely unknowable, hidden and remote—to prevent them, in fact, from being in any real sense *observable*. On the other hand, by accepting phenomenalism, we seem to rob them of all their substance, to give them an outrageously 'shadowy', 'attenuated' existence, if not to dispense with them altogether.

It is my opinion, however, that we may safely opt for the first of these alternatives. For I hope to show that the difficulties which this involves may all be overcome. In Section IV, I shall give an account of perception that will depict the physical world as something altogether different from our sense-data while at the same time doing, as I hope, full justice to the seeming 'directness' of our 'contact' with it. And in Section V, I shall endeavour to show how, on this view, our beliefs about physical objects may be justified. I shall in due course mention, and I hope dispose of, two further arguments which have sometimes been brought against any 'realist' account of the physical world.[1] If I succeed in these various undertakings, then it would seem that I shall have adequately disposed of phenomenalism. For we shall be left without a single motive for embracing what is intrinsically a highly unplausible doctrine. I should like, however, before embarking on this programme, to set forth what has always seemed to me a decisive argument against it.

Given any statement concerning some matter of fact, of the sort that admits of truth or falsity, it is evident that if it is true, the

---

[1] These are (i) the argument that we could never form any *conception* of a set of objects wholly distinct from all possible experiences and (ii) the argument that we could never teach a child the meaning of any words used to describe such objects (see Section IV, pp. 106–19).

world must be in some way different—either in the past, present, future or a combination of these—from what it would be if the statement were false (and *vice versa*). (I shall speak of the world as 'being' different, in the past, present or future, as a shorthand for saying that it either has been different, is different or will be different.) Now this difference must be an actual difference. And this applies even if the statement in question is a 'counterfactual' hypothetical statement, i.e. one stating what *would* be the case if the world were in some way other than it is. Regardless of what the statement may be, there must be some actual difference between the case where it is true and the case where it is false. If there is no actual difference between these two cases, then there is no difference between them at all. And if this be so, then there is no way in which the statement can be true or false.

Consider now two possible worlds in one of which some counterfactual hypothetical statement is true, while in the other it is false. That is, it is true in the one world, but false in the other, that in certain conditions not actually obtaining in either world something or other would be the case. In order for this to be so, these two worlds must in some way differ from one another. And this difference must be an actual difference. But this means that something must actually exist or occur in the one which does not exist or occur in the other—in short, something or other must *be* the case in the one which is not the case in the other. For it is senseless to distinguish them by saying that there are, in only one of them, certain 'hypothetical' things or events. As I remarked above,[1] a thing that would exist is not a thing that does exist; and equally, a thing that would occur is not a thing that does occur. If nothing actually existed or occurred in the one world which did not also exist or occur in the other, then nothing at all would exist or occur in one only; and hence the two would be indistinguishable. And were this so, then any statement whatever which was true in the one would, *ipso facto*, be true in the other.

There is no paradox here. Suppose it is true in the one world that the only man answering to a certain description would be six-feet tall were he two inches taller than he is. And suppose this

[1] P. 61.

is false of the only man answering to the same description in the other world. Plainly there is something which actually exists in only one of these worlds; for plainly there exists in only one of them a man answering to this description who is five-feet ten inches tall. But suppose it is true in the one world, false in the other, that the only glass answering to a certain description would break if it fell. In this case it is less obvious what, exactly, must exist or occur in only one world. Perhaps there exists in only one a glass (answering to this description) which possesses a certain structure. But whether or not we *know* in what precise way these worlds differ from one another, they cannot be identical.

Now, according to phenomenalism, any statement about a physical object depends for its truth solely on a set of facts, infinite in number, about sense-data. And what constitutes the majority of these is the fact that certain sense-data would exist if certain conditions were fulfilled. The question therefore arises: given any true statement which expresses a fact of this sort, what actually exists or occurs which would not do so were this statement false? How is any such statement to be 'categorically under-pinned'?

The phenomenalist cannot brush this question aside by saying (as some philosophers have done) that counterfactual hypothetical statements are not statements in such a sense that they must be true or false. For it is essential to his thesis that the *truth* of an ordinary statement about a physical object requires the *truth* of an infinity of counterfactual hypotheticals about sense-data. Phenomenalism is precisely an account of the truth-conditions of any statement about a physical object; and it is beside the point in this connection that any such conditions are infinite in number and therefore incapable of exhaustive specification. Accordingly, given any true statement to the effect that certain sense-data would exist if certain conditions were fulfilled, the world must be in some way different from what it would be were this statement false. If there is no such difference, then there is no way in which the statement can be true or false. And if no statement of this sort can be true or false, then neither can any statement about a physical object.

The problem of 'underpinning' almost *any* counterfactual hypothetical statement is, for a number of reasons, a notoriously difficult one; and I do not propose to discuss it in general terms. But it can be shown, without such a discussion, that the phenomenalist makes no conceivable allowance for the underpinning of counterfactual hypotheticals about sense-data. The reason for this is that he does not have enough categorical material at his disposal. He would be obliged to give an account of the underpinning of such statements which did away with any reference to physical objects, since in his view these are themselves to be analyzed in terms of those very statements of which the account is to be given. The question, therefore, which he has to ask himself is this: Given the truth of any such statement, how is the (actual) *mental* world—which for him is the complete world—in any way different from what it would be were this statement false? What mental entities actually exist (in the past, present or future) which would not exist were it false? If there is no possible answer to this question, then there can be no difference *whatever*, on the phenomenalist view, between the case where any such statement is true and the case where it is false. And if this be so, then equally, given any statement about a physical object, there can be no difference whatever between the truth and falsity of *this* statement.

No very elaborate argument is needed to show that this is indeed the position in which the phenomenalist lands himself. We can simplify the question before us by asking: Given the truth of any statement about a physical object, what mental entities actually exist which would not exist were it false? If this question is unanswerable, then it is no use saying that certain sense-data are *obtainable* which would not be obtainable were it false. Consider first any true statement about a physical object which is, in fact, perceived. Because it is perceived, we may say that certain sense-data are experienced which, very likely, would not be experienced were the statement false. But to say this is not enough, precisely because we have to include the words 'very likely'. For *whatever* sense-data are actually experienced, it is at least logically possible that all of the very same sense-data would still be experienced were the statement false—on account, perhaps, of a large-scale hallucination.[1] And indeed, whatever experiences of *any* kind (perceptual or otherwise) are actually undergone, it is possible that these would all be undergone were the statement false. The phenomenalist himself says, in effect, just this when he says that no statement about a physical object can ever be 'conclusively verified'. That is, no amount or kind of actual experiences can ever ensure the truth of any statement about a physical object. But this is all that my argument requires; for it means that if phenomenalism is correct, then at least there *need* be no difference between the truth and falsity of any such statement: the absence of any difference is at least a possibility. And if this applies even where the object referred to is perceived, it applies more plainly still where it is not. And since in fact there *must* be some difference between the truth and falsity of such a statement, phenomenalism cannot be correct.

The matter could be expressed in another way. As the phenomenalist concedes, no amount of actual experiences can ever ensure the truth of any statement about a physical object. Whatever ones are undergone, it is consistent with their being so both that the statement is true and also that it is false. What further determines its truth or falsity is the truth or falsity of certain counterfactual hypothetical statements about sense-data. But in the phenomenalist's universe, there can be nothing to decide as between these two possibilities. For by hypothesis, the world is identical in either case.

The fact is, it is quite impossible to give an account of the 'underpinning' of counterfactual hypotheticals about sense-data without some reference to physical objects. And only the 'realist' is at liberty to make any such reference. To put the point in a nutshell: what sense-data would be experienced in any given set of conditions depends not only on what those conditions are, but also on *what physical object is so situated that it would be perceived upon their fulfilment*—as well as on the physiological state of the percipient. Or it may depend on the latter only, bearing in mind the possibility of hallucination.

The phenomenalist programme, therefore, of 'reducing' the physical to the mental is simply not feasible.

[1] See above, pp. 56–7.

For my part, I find this argument virtually conclusive.[1] The only way I can think of in which it could conceivably be met would be to allow that statements about physical objects are neither true nor false—which would amount to saying that no single region of space either is or is not occupied by physical objects of any given sorts. If this is the price we have to pay for phenomenalism, it is an extremely heavy one. At the very least, no one will want to pay this price unless he has some overwhelmingly powerful motive for accepting phenomenalism. But I hope in the following two sections to rid him of any such motive. For I hope to show that the arguments for phenomenalism are one and all invalid. And should anyone persist in maintaining a phenomenalist position, then it is reasonable to assume not just that my refutation of these arguments has failed to satisfy him, but, on the contrary, that he considers at least one of them so utterly *conclusive* as to force him to the wildly paradoxical conclusion just mentioned. The acceptance of an argument, moreover, involves the acceptance of its premiss. And it will not do if the truth of this premiss is less self-evident than is the falsity of some conclusion to which it leads. And I hope to make it plain that the premisses of all the arguments concerned are at least open to question.

The principles underlying them are, in fact, so deeply engrained in the modern empiricist tradition that it has become common practice simply to take them for granted. But if phenomenalism with its unpalatable corollaries is forced upon one by these deeply-rooted principles, then the time has come to subject them to a process of doubt. And if we see fit to abandon them, we shall not be flouting the one fundamental empiricist tenet which really is self-evident, namely that all our knowledge about the world is derived, and can only be derived, from experience. For in adopting a realist view of physical objects according to which they are something wholly distinct from all possible experiences, we are not overlooking the obvious fact that only by experiencing sense-data can we *find out* that any such object exists. What we are

---

[1] I must remind the reader, however, that it is by no means solely on the strength of this argument that I would have him reject phenomenalism (see above, p. 62).

rejecting are certain additional assumptions which have long been supposed to follow from this fact.

I conclude that phenomenalism can be discarded without further ado, subject at least to our failure to find any overpowering motive for accepting it together with its consequences. To the question 'What is a physical object if it is not what the phenomenalist says it is?' we cannot at this stage make any particularly illuminating reply. For *whatever* characteristics we may ascribe to it, the phenomenalist professes to do the same. But there is no unfathomable mystery here. We have but to reflect on the character of our perceptual experiences. Of what sort are the objects 'presented' to us by our sense-data? This is something known to us all. I suggest, even, that careful reflection on this should really be sufficient to persuade anyone that phenomenalism is false. For it seems to me manifest that the objects so 'presented' to us are of a sort different from what the phenomenalist would have us believe. Each is a solid, unified, three-dimensional being literally existing 'out there'.

Nevertheless, while everyone knows what a physical object is, I agree that the problem still remains of analyzing this, and in particular of analyzing its relationship with sense-data. I shall set forth my views on this in the following section.

Having rejected phenomenalism, we must now acknowledge a small element of truth that it contains.[1]

I have drawn attention already[2] to the striking 'vividness' with which sense-data, and in particular visual sense-data, 'present' to us those objects that we are said to perceive, so that they *seem* actually to have become part of our experience. And I have said, in connection with this, that the ordinary percipient is not conscious of his visual sense-data as being anything different from the physical objects they 'present'. This means that he draws no clear distinction between the visual appearance of an object and the object itself. It is not, therefore, in the least surprising that certain

[1] All of the main points which I am about to make are discussed more fully in the following section.
[2] Section II, pp. 51–2.

salient features of the visual appearances of things come to be ascribed by him to the things themselves. And the most important feature in this category is colour. If an object is (normally) visually 'presented' to him by a red sense-datum, then he says not just that this object *looks* red, but that it *is* red.

And this brings me to my point about the grain of truth in phenomenalism. It is that *some* of those properties which we habitually ascribe to physical objects are to be analyzed in phenomenal terms, that is in terms of their appearances. To say 'The table next door is brown' may be taken to mean: The table next door normally[1] looks brown (or would look brown) to a human observer, or in other words it normally is or would be visually 'presented' to such an observer by a brown sense-datum.[2] My reason for saying this is merely that I cannot understand what is meant by describing an object as brown except by reference to the relevant sense-data. Indeed it seems quite obvious that being

[1] I insert this word to allow for the fact that a thing which normally looks brown may sometimes look some other colour, for example in unusual lighting conditions or to a person who is colour-blind or who is suffering from jaundice or who has taken certain drugs. Because the thing looks a different colour in these cases from what it usually does, and because we know that the sole reason for its doing so is the presence of these unusual conditions rather than any change in the thing itself, we come, by a natural psychological process, to say that in these conditions it looks some colour other than its 'real' colour.

It seems to me misguided of those philosophers who have attempted to classify these conditions by reference to certain characteristics which they share rather than to the mere fact of their uncommonness. It is precisely because they are relatively uncommon that we ascribe colour to physical objects in the way we do. If all of them were constantly recurring, with the result that any physical object looked a multitude of different colours from moment to moment, our attention would, I suspect, thereby be drawn to the fact that our visual sense-data are something different from the physical objects they 'present'; and it is because, as things are, we fail to differentiate between them that we think of physical objects as being coloured. (We are not led to differentiate between them merely by discovering that in certain conditions an object looks a different colour from what it usually does. For while we say that in these conditions the colour it looks is different from the colour it is, it does not occur to us, provided they remain sufficiently uncommon, that the former *is* the colour of something *else*.)

[2] Besides ascribing colour to physical objects, we speak also of certain kinds of *things* consisting solely in certain patterns of colour (or of black and white) and therefore analyzable solely in terms of visual sense-data—e.g. pictures, written words, shadows, rainbows.

brown and normally looking brown amount to the same thing.

On the other hand, it is essential to my 'realist' position that the shape and size of physical objects are not to be analyzed in this way. I most certainly do find intelligible the notion of a three-dimensional object existing independently of all sense-data and whose spatial properties are not definable in sensory terms. I *can* understand what is meant by describing an object as round or small without any reference to sense-data. But further, we have established that a physical object *must* exist independently of sense-data; and for this to be so it must have *some* properties not analyzable in terms of them. And were we to exclude its shape and size from this category, then nothing of the object would still remain. It is of the very essence of a physical object that it is three-dimensionally extended, that it occupies a volume, and not merely a point, of space. And this means that the concept of a physical object is inseparable from that of an object having a specific three-dimensional shape and size. On the other hand, it is possible, as I shall show presently,[1] to dissociate the concept of a physical object from the property of being coloured. And therefore, while the realist may take a 'phenomenalistic' view of colour, to take such a view of shape or size would involve the abandonment of his realism. I might add that, in view of the number of philosophers who have regarded phenomenalism as an affront to common sense, it can hardly be thought *obvious*, by contrast with what I have just said about colour, that to describe an object's shape or size is to describe its appearance. On the contrary, it seems to me, as it does to numerous others who have not been tainted by phenomenalism, as obvious that its shape or size cannot be analyzed in terms of sense-data as that its colour must be so analyzed. It goes without saying too that the same applies to its position, since this is constituted by its spatial relations to other objects.

Besides colour, there are other properties which, more obviously still, do require sensory analysis. These comprise all properties of sound, smell and taste together with certain properties of touch, such as heat and cold. What, for example, do I mean

[1] Pp. 72–8.

by saying that a lump of sugar *is* sweet if not that it normally *tastes* (or would taste) sweet? Equally, it is not the case that shape, size and position are the sole properties not calling for such analysis. We shall note various others shortly.[1]

The distinction which I am here drawing is the same, in essence, as that drawn by Locke[2] between what he called 'primary' and 'secondary' qualities. And doubtless its validity will be questioned. Surely, it will be said, there cannot be this fundamental difference between the way a thing is round and the way it is red. It may be pointed out that sense-data are themselves shaped as well as coloured; so that is it not quite arbitrarily that I regard the shapedness of these as somehow corresponding, in a way their colour does not, with a non-sensory character of physical objects?[3]

I shall, however, defer any further discussion of this topic until the following section, when I shall aim to show what is the precise relationship between sense-data and physical objects, thus explaining how and to what extent the one 'corresponds' in character with the other. I shall content myself here with the following brief remarks. Given that our sense-data 'present' to us something other than themselves, which must therefore have certain non-sensory properties, and given that we habitually confound the one with the other, *it is only to be expected* that certain features of our sense-data will come to be ascribed by us to the things they 'present'. It is only to be expected too that we shall be wholly unaware that physical objects have two distinct kinds of properties, sensory and non-sensory.

I should not want to say, as Locke sometimes did, that we are

---

[1] Pp. 73–4.

[2] *Vide* John Locke, *An Essay concerning Human Understanding*, Book II, ch. 8.

[3] Locke himself distinguished between the 'primary' and 'secondary' qualities of physical objects on the ground that our perception of the latter depends in part on the conditions of observation (such as the lighting or the state of the observer) and may vary as they vary. But this is certainly not a valid ground, since our perception of the 'primary' qualities is equally dependent on such conditions. I do not, however, for one moment believe that Locke was initially persuaded of this distinction by any of those arguments with which he supports it. I believe that he found merely, as I have, that the idea of non-sensory colour, unlike that of non-sensory shape, is unintelligible. And having found this, he thereupon searched for arguments to prove it.

mistaken in ascribing colour to physical objects, that they are really colourless, that our visual sense-data alone are coloured. This is not what is implied by *equating* an object's colour with the colour it looks. We can allow, nevertheless, that there is a sense—an obvious sense—in which a philosopher may distinguish those properties (such as shape) which belong to physical objects 'intrinsically' from those (such as colour) which do not. And having made this distinction, we may then be tempted to say that most of us mistakenly believe that objects are 'intrinsically' coloured no less than they are 'intrinsically' shaped. I think, however, that this would be inaccurate much as it would be inaccurate to say that we mistakenly identify our visual sense-data with the objects they 'present'.[1] It would be to credit us with an exaggerated profoundness. We do indeed believe, say, that grass is green, which it is. But the question of whether its greenness is or is not an 'intrinsic' property, in the special sense here in question, is simply not one normally ever raised, save by the philosopher.

Still, just as it can be said that we *fail to differentiate between* our visual sense-data and the objects they 'present', it can be said too that we recognize no difference between the way these objects are coloured and the way they are shaped. We rightly think of physical objects as something wholly distinct from any of our experiences; and it does not occur to us that certain of the properties we ascribe to them are in fact analyzable in terms of experiences (our experiences of sense-data). But nor, on the other hand, are we actually of the opinion that they are not.

Finally, we must examine an argument used by Armstrong[2]—and derived by him from Berkeley and Hume—to establish that the 'intrinsic' properties of a physical object must include at least one of those, such as colour, which I say are not intrinsic. What he tries to show is that the notion of a physical object would otherwise be indistinguishable from that of a vacuum, or region of empty space. He first examines, one by one, the list of primary qualities proposed by Descartes, together with the one

[1] See Section II, pp. 51–2.
[2] D. M. Armstrong, *Perception and the Physical World*, Part V, ch. 15.

addition made to this list by Locke, and argues that none of these would serve to differentiate a physical object from a vacuum.

Descartes's list[1] consists of shape, size, position, duration, movability, divisibility and number. However, Armstrong says (rightly) that '*number* is an interloper here. A physical object has not got a number in the way it has a shape, size, position, duration and velocity. It makes sense to say that an object is round or at rest, but it makes no sense to say that it is three. Only if we say that it is three pounds in weight, or made of three pieces of wood, do we have an intelligible assertion. Only when we have *specified a unit* does our attribution of number become meaningful. So to speak of physical objects as having number is not really to characterize their nature at all'. The question, therefore, is whether the remaining properties in this list suffice to distinguish a physical object from a vacuum.

Armstrong takes first the properties of shape, size and duration. And he points out that all of these are possessed by a vacuum no less than by a physical object.

Next, position. But this is a relational property. The position of a physical object is constituted by its spatial relations to *other physical objects*. It cannot, therefore, on pain of circularity, serve as the required differentiating mark. The notion of position presupposes the notion of a physical object.

'It might seem', Armstrong goes on, 'that motion would be a sufficient differentiating mark to distinguish between physical objects and mere empty space. For although a physical object is capable of motion, it is not clear what, if anything, the motion of an empty space would come to. But what is motion? A body is in motion if it is in a series of adjoining places at successive times. That is all that motion is. (Similarly, rest is simply being at the same place at successive times.) Now this means that we can give an analysis of motion solely in terms of the concepts of shape, size, position and duration. It is not a new primitive concept. But we have already examined these concepts, and have found that, even when they are taken together, they are insufficient to differentiate physical objects from empty space. We will still want to know

---

[1] *Vide* René Descartes, *Meditations on the First Philosophy*, Meditation V.

what is the nature of that which is in a series of adjoining places during successive times.'

There remains the property of divisibility. But, Armstrong points out, 'to say a thing is divisible is to say that it is capable of being broken up or separated into two or more *things*. Clearly, this will not serve to define, or help to define, the nature of a thing, any more than it will help to define a cat to say it is the offspring of two cats'.

To Descartes's list of primary qualities Locke added that of 'solidity'.[1] By this he means the 'resistance . . . in body [i.e. a physical object] to the entrance of any other body into the place it possesses, till it has left it'. And therefore, once again, this notion presupposes the notion of a physical object.

Finally, Armstrong examines certain other properties which Descartes or Locke might have added.[2] But he finds, as we should expect, that all of them are either analyzable in terms of the Cartesian-Lockean list or are relations which one physical object has to others.

He concludes, as I have said, that in order for a physical object to be distinguishable from a vacuum, any list of its 'intrinsic' properties must contain some such property as colour.

The answer to this argument is hinted at by Armstrong himself when he remarks how it might be pointed out that the notion of a vacuum is 'logically subsequent to the objects that environ it'. But he goes on: 'This is true, but not to the point. Granting this, we do, or could, speak of the shape, size and duration of both physical objects and vacua. (For instance, we could teach a child what length was by comparing different distances between physical things, even though those distances were vacuous.) So if physical objects are more than vacua they must have some *further* property to differentiate them.'

But the fact that a vacuum is 'logically subsequent to the objects that environ it' is very much to the point. Not merely do

---

[1] *Vide* John Locke, *An Essay concerning Human Understanding*, Book II, ch. 4.
[2] For some examples of such properties, see Section IV of this book, pp. 123–4. (My own examples do not include all of those given by Armstrong, but they will serve equally well.)

these objects *enter into* the definition of a vacuum. It is definable *exclusively* in terms of them. It is nothing over and above them, in short it is 'logically constructed' from them. Before discussing the relevance of this to Armstrong's argument, I must first explain how it is 'constructed'. Let us, for convenience, think of the objects enclosing a vacuum as a single composite object having a single composite shape and size.

To say of a certain object that it encloses a vacuum is to say, firstly, that it does *not* enclose any physical object. (It is not to say that it *does* enclose something *other than* a physical object having a separate existence.) Secondly, it is to say that it is of such a shape that it *could* enclose a physical object—and 'enclose' must here be taken to mean 'completely enclose'. It is possible for one physical object completely to enclose another only if the former is of such a shape as may be described by saying that it has a 'continuous' inner surface. The kind of shape I mean is exemplified by that of a sealed tin, which can and often does completely enclose some other physical object. If, on the other hand, its shape as a whole is altered by the act of piercing it, then it can no longer do so; for while it can still be said to have an inner surface, this is now 'interrupted' at the point where it has been pierced. And plainly it cannot be said to enclose a vacuum just because it could not and therefore does not completely enclose any physical object.

An object can be said, therefore, to enclose a vacuum if it does not, but is so shaped that it could, enclose a physical object. And I should make clear the following point. While it must be *capable* of *completely* enclosing a physical object, there must be none which it *actually* encloses either completely *or even partially*—by which I mean that there must be none adjoining any part of its inner surface.

It remains for me to show how the properties ascribable to any given vacuum are 'constructed' from those of the object which encloses it.

To say of a certain object that the vacuum it encloses has a certain *shape and size* is to say that if there *were* a physical object which it completely enclosed, this object *would* have the shape and size in question. To be more precise, we must qualify the words 'physical object' with the words 'having no inner surface'. For were the enclosed object itself to have an inner surface, it would define the shape and size only of one region of the total vacuum. The 'categorical underpinning' of the counterfactual hypothetical statement here concerned presents no problems. For the shape and size that this object *would* have depend solely on (are deducible from) the *actual* shape and size of the enclosing object, i.e. that said to enclose a vacuum.

In addition, the *position* which the enclosed object would have, that is the spatial relations which it would have to other physical objects, serves to define the position of the vacuum.

Finally, one and the same vacuum can be said to *endure* through time for as long as it retains approximately the same shape, size and position—there being, of course, no precise answer to the question how far these would have to alter before it ceased to be the same vacuum.

I believe that I am now in a position to meet Armstrong's argument.

Quite simply, a physical object and a vacuum can be distinguished from one another by saying that while a vacuum (being nothing over and above the physical object which encloses it) is a 'logical construction', a physical object, on the other hand, is not: it is something which exists 'in its own right'.[1] If they are different from one another in this way, then neither of them is indistinguishable from the other. And therefore no further difference between them is needed to distinguish them.

But this may appear too easy a solution: it may well be felt inadequate until I have explained more fully why Armstrong's reasoning is fallacious.

The assumption on which his argument rests is that in order for a physical object to be distinguishable from a vacuum, its intrinsic properties must include at least one property not included in those

[1] It is, I suspect, this fact which Armstrong is trying to state when he speaks at one point of the 'substantiality' of a physical object. For reasons which will shortly become apparent, he disclaims the perfectly correct view that this constitutes the required differentiating mark. But he nevertheless concludes with the words: 'Perhaps, behind the problems of knowledge we have been investigating, lies the deeper problem of *substance*' (my italics).

of a vacuum. This assumption is deemed self-evident; and it may well appear so. But as thus expressed, it is exposed to an ambiguity of interpretation. It is a correct assumption if and only if (a) it is taken to mean that the intrinsic properties of a physical object must include at least one property not included in the *intrinsic* properties of a vacuum, and (b) the words 'intrinsic property' are defined in a certain way, namely as follows:

A given thing possesses a given property 'intrinsically' provided that the possession of that property by that thing requires for its analysis no reference to anything other than the thing itself.

If, on the other hand, the assumption is taken to mean that the intrinsic properties of a physical object must include at least one property not possessed *at all* by a vacuum (intrinsically or non-intrinsically), then it is false, as I shall now show.

The above definition of the words 'intrinsic property' has the following all-important consequence: that a vacuum, being a 'logical construction', has, and can have, no intrinsic properties whatever. For its properties are all of them 'constructed' from, and therefore analyzable in terms of, something other than itself, namely the object which encloses it. In order to show, therefore, that a physical object is distinguishable from a vacuum, no more is required than to name *any* one intrinsic property of a physical object. And this affords me no difficulty. Let us take the property of shape. This (on a 'realist' view of the physical world) is certainly an intrinsic property of physical objects. An object's shape requires for its analysis no reference to anything other than the object itself: it is not analyzable in terms of sense-data nor is it a relation which the object has to other objects. Given this, and given also that a vacuum can have no intrinsic properties, it follows that it is logically impossible that any physical object should also be a vacuum (and *vice versa*). And since this follows from these two facts alone, it does not require the further supposition that a physical object has any intrinsic property not possessed at all by a vacuum, either intrinsically or non-intrinsically. And it is on this unwarranted supposition that Armstrong's argument is based.

It is easy to see how he came to make this supposition. First, he assumed rightly that it must be possible so to define the notion of a physical object as to preclude the possibility that any physical object should also be a vacuum. He assumed also, again rightly, that since a physical object is not a 'logical construction', it must be possible to define it solely in terms of its intrinsic properties—that is, without mentioning any of its properties that are analyzable either in terms of sense-data or in terms of *anything* other than itself. And from these two correct assumptions he inferred that the properties figuring in such a definition must include at least one not possessable (at all) by a vacuum. But this conclusion does not follow. For, while it is possible to define a physical object solely in terms of its intrinsic properties, it is not enough merely that all the properties in question should *in fact* belong to a physical object intrinsically. If the definition is to be complete, that they do so belong must be *incorporated into it*. In other words, a physical object must be defined not merely as a thing possessing properties X, Y, Z, but as a thing possessing intrinsic properties X, Y, Z. It stands to reason that since a physical object is not a 'logical construction', its definition must be such as to preclude it from so being. That is, it must be so defined as to preclude the possibility that all of its properties should be non-intrinsic (i.e. analyzable in terms of something else). And any definition which meets this requirement will automatically ensure that no physical object can also be a vacuum.

I conclude, then, that no reason has been found why a physical object's intrinsic properties should include such a property as colour.

IV

IN CONTACT WITH THE PHYSICAL WORLD

Our awareness of the physical world depends, as we have observed, on Nature's ingenious device whereby physical objects are, in some remarkable manner, 'presented' to our minds by our sense-data. In this section, I shall undertake to explain how, in my view, this 'presentative function' is performed. To do this, I shall have to propose an answer to the old question: What are the relations between sense-data and the physical objects they 'present'?

To begin with, I have no wish to question the orthodox scientific view of the way in which our perceptual experiences are *causally related* to the physical objects we are said to perceive. I accept unreservedly the familiar account given by the physiologist of the complex causal chain of events involved in, for example, seeing something: how light is transmitted from the object to our eyes, from which impulses travel to our brain, and finally culminate in our visual experience.[1] But of course, this does not explain at all how sense-data 'present' physical objects to our consciousness in the way they do.[2] On the contrary, it makes it harder to

[1] But how can the physiologist possibly *know* that perceptual experiences are caused by objects which, according to me, are something wholly distinct from all possible experiences? For any scientific discovery can be made only on the strength of a certain set of observations, and these can consist only in certain perceptual experiences on the part of the scientist. This being so, how can any number of such observations, whatever form they may take, entitle him to postulate 'external' objects as the causes of perceptual experiences? This question is commonly thought by philosophers to be an unanswerable one. Since, however, they are reluctant to disavow the scientist's discoveries, they conclude that what he thus refers to as the 'causes' of our experiences must themselves really be analyzable in terms of experiences. And this conclusion opens up one route whereby they are led to a phenomenalist view of the physical world. I shall, however, endeavour to show, first, that we can rightly be said to *observe* (and not merely to 'postulate') 'external' objects, and secondly, that there is no good reason why such observation should not afford us genuine knowledge of them.

[2] Though we shall see, in Section VI, that there is something *else* which it does help to explain.

understand this in view of the large number of links in the causal chain by which any sense-datum is separated from the physical object it serves to 'present'. In order, therefore, to explain how this 'presentative function' is performed, we must find some further relationship between them—some relationship other than a causal one.

My view is that the relationship in question is that of *symbol* to *thing symbolized*. Since, as we have discovered, it is logically impossible for us to gain 'immediate access' to the physical world (any experience that we have being necessarily something totally separate and distinct from any physical object), the processes of evolution have been obliged to devise a *language* for the purpose of conveying information to us about our physical environment—a language whose symbols, in contrast to that which they symbolize (i.e. physical objects), are things of such a sort as to constitute features of our *experience*. And they have 'invented' to this end the language of sense-data.

Before elaborating further on this, I should say a few words on the general matter of conveying information by means of symbols. Anything that contains information through functioning as a symbol performs its symbolic function in virtue of a convention (or set of conventions). The performance of this function cannot depend solely on its intrinsic properties. Consider a case where it might be tempting to think otherwise—a case where a symbol resembles an object whose existence it symbolizes, for example the road sign consisting of a drawing of a level-crossing gate. It is clearly not a matter of convention that this drawing bears some resemblance in its shape to an actual level-crossing gate. But it *is* a matter of convention that it serves to symbolize the existence of an object so resembling it. Not all road signs are governed by the convention that they are to symbolize the existence of an object resembling them. There are some that are governed by other conventions. The sign [P] for instance, bears no resemblance to the parking area whose existence it symbolizes.

Since, therefore, sense-data are symbols serving to convey information, they must perforce symbolize what they do symbolize

—viz. the existence of physical objects of particular kinds—in virtue of a set of conventions, the conventions that go to make the sense-datum language the language that it is.[1] The nature of these conventions we shall consider in due course. However, we must note here and now that the conventions of the sense-datum language differ in one all-important respect from those of other languages. The conventions of, for example, the English language are man-made. And in order to understand this language, a person has to *learn* to interpret its symbols correctly in accordance with these conventions. The conventions of the sense-datum language, on the other hand, are the artifice not of man, but of Nature[2]—no doubt they were gradually developed and refined over a long period of evolution. Nature has contrived, moreover—again thanks to evolution—that we do not need to learn her language, as we do any man-made language, but are born with the innate power to understand it,[3] that is to interpret its symbols (i.e. sense-data) correctly in accordance with its conventions.

[1] It is frequently taken for granted that any philosopher who holds a 'realist' view of physical objects must be advocating what is known as 'the representative theory of perception'. By this is meant the theory—of which the best-known exponent is Locke—that perceiving physical objects consists in referring one's sense-data to 'external' objects of which they are themselves resembling (or partially resembling) 'copies' or 'representations'. But it should be clear from what I have just said that I am not advocating this theory, at any rate in its common form. For, even were sense-data to bear some resemblance to physical objects, I should still not maintain that it is or that it could be in any way *because of* such resemblance that they serve to inform us about the physical world—any more than a drawing of a level-crossing gate serves to inform us about such a gate *because of* its resemblance to it. If I am to be said to hold the view that our sense-data 'represent' physical objects, I do so not in that sense of this word in which a drawing 'represents' whatever it is a drawing of, but in that sense in which a symbol 'represents' whatever it serves to symbolize *whether or not* it in fact resembles it at all.

[2] For this reason, the whole notion of the sense-datum 'language' necessarily involves the personification of Nature, a fact which may lead the reader to regard it with some suspicion. I shall, however, attempt to justify this feature of it at a later stage (pp. 87–90).

[3] It is often assumed that any philosopher who adopts the view that we have any such 'innate' powers of understanding thereby automatically forfeits all claim to be taken seriously. For it is alleged that any view of this kind runs counter to certain unassailable principles of *empiricism*. I shall, however, eventually discuss these principles at length (pp. 106–18), when I shall aim to show, in the first place, that my denial of empiricism is nothing like as far-reaching as it may appear

Nature has had no option *but to* contrive our innate understanding of the sense-datum language, as it would be impossible for us to acquire an understanding of it simply *by experience*.[1] For since the physical objects whose existence sense-data serve to symbolize are something totally distinct from all possible experiences, we could never learn from experience alone to associate sense-data of any kind with physical objects of any kind: experience alone could teach us only to associate sense-data of one kind with sense-data of another kind, which, since we have rejected phenomenalism, would not in itself enable us even to form any conception of, let alone any beliefs about, the physical world.

I say we could never learn from experience *alone* to associate sense-data of any kind with physical objects of any kind. It is obvious that having once begun to interpret sense-data correctly in terms of physical objects, as the result of our innate capacity to do so, we can then learn, by experience, to extract more information about the physical world from any given sense-datum or set of sense-data than would have been possible without the relevant experience. To take an extreme example, we can learn to infer the existence of a complete church with a spire from a distant view of only the very tip of a spire. Our innate understanding of the sense-datum language would *of course* not by itself have enabled us to interpret any visual sense-datum constituting such a view in terms of a complete church. In general, we can learn by experience to identify physical objects of particular kinds on the basis of sense-data which could not otherwise have enabled us so to identify them. Such is our ability to profit from past experience that a single view of almost any object we are likely to encounter en-

to be, and secondly, that while there is admittedly one widely accepted principle which I do deny, those who subscribe to it do so for entirely invalid reasons.

[1] This impossibility serves to clarify what I mean in calling our understanding of the sense-datum language 'innate'. It is innate *as opposed to* learnt by experience (i.e. 'innate' *means:* not learnt by experience). I am not, therefore, implying that the new-born infant necessarily interprets its sense-data correctly in terms of physical objects from the very first moments of its life. I leave open the question, which rests within the province of the empirical psychologist, whether any period of time has to elapse before its innate power to understand the sense-datum language *first begins to manifest itself.*

ables us to make a more detailed identification of the object than would have been possible without this experience. Nor does experience enable us only to make *qualitative* identifications that we should otherwise have been unable to make. It enables us also to make *numerical* identifications. Indeed in every case where there is a time-gap, however small, between two occasions on which we perceive what we identify as the very same object, we rely for this identification in some measure on our past experience: we rely on it for a variety of assumptions on which this identification depends. To give a simple example of just one way in which we rely on it: if we close our eyes for a second in the course of gazing at some object and take it for granted that the object we see on re-opening them is the very same one, it is only on the strength of our past experience that we can know that an object of the kind in question is *not* liable to behave like, say, a hailstone and at any moment melt to be forthwith replaced by an object qualitatively identical with it.

The ways in which experience contributes to our ability to identify physical objects (qualitatively and numerically) are, in-deed, both extremely varied and extremely complex; and much space has been devoted to discussing them by philosophers and psychologists alike. But since we have rejected phenomenalism, we cannot accept the view that experience alone is responsible for this ability. On the contrary, we must say that experience alone could not enable us to identify physical objects at all. Without an innate capacity to interpret sense-data in terms of physical objects, we could never even know that there *were* any physical objects. Perceiving physical objects involves interpreting certain features of our experiences—sense-data—in terms of things that are distinct from all possible experiences, and no amount of experience could by itself enable us to do this. Experience can do no more than enable us to perceive *in greater detail*, in the sense of enabling us to learn more about the physical world from any given sense-data than would have been possible solely through our innate under-standing of the sense-datum language.

How much information this innate understanding alone enables us to extract from any given sense-data, and to what extent we have to be 'helped out' by experience, will become clearer when we examine the nature of the conventions governing the sense-datum language.[1] But it will help if I mention straightaway that it is only visual and tactual sense-data which constitute the symbols of this language (and therefore only these which are governed by *conventions*): given our innate ability to interpret these correctly in terms of physical objects of particular kinds, it is through experience *alone* that we come to associate sense-data belonging to the *other* senses with physical objects of particular sorts.

I am all too well aware that my account as presented thus far could scarcely be better calculated to evoke the derision of modern philosophers. Before proceeding any further, however, let me remind the reader of an objection often brought to bear against *any* 'realist' account of perception.[2] I stated this objection in Section III.[3] It is, that to regard physical objects as something wholly distinct from all possible experiences is to prevent them from being in any real sense *observable*. In supposing that physical objects exist over and above all sense-data, we are said to have erected an impenetrable 'iron curtain' of sense-data between us and the physical world: we become 'cut off from' this world in a way that flatly contradicts the manifest *awareness* of it with which our senses provide us.

I suggested, it will be remembered,[4] that phenomenalism and realism *each* appears at first sight to inflict a grave injury on common sense. Phenomenalism, I said, in supposing that there exists the totality of experience and nothing at all else *in addition*, appears to paint a picture of the universe that is grossly incomplete. However skilfully the phenomenalist may state his case, one is inevitably left with the impression that he is rendering no more than lip-service to the existence of physical objects. The realist, on the other hand, by accepting the common-sense view of the nature of physical objects, thereby lands himself with the seem-

[1] Pp. 123-32.
[2] I shall discuss other objections to any such account later (see pp. 106-19 of this section, and the whole of Section V).
[3] See pp. 61-2.
[4] Ibid.

ingly insuperable problem of giving an account in line with common sense of the nature of perceptual awareness.

I nevertheless expressed the belief that while the phenomenalist's breach with common sense is unhealable, realism and common sense are in truth reconcilable with one another. I gave at the time no indication of how this reconciliation is possible, but said: 'I shall give an account of perception that will depict the physical world as something altogether different from our sense-data while at the same time doing, as I hope, full justice to the seeming "directness" of our "contact" with it'.[1]

I am aware, however, that it may be quite unclear from my account so far how I can make good this promise. For while I have given some explanation of how sense-data supply us with knowledge about the physical world, I have yet to show in what sense this knowledge could possibly be described as anything but second hand. My description of sense-data (or rather visual and tactual sense-data) as information-conveying symbols seems to imply that they merely *tell us* about the physical world, much as the road sign consisting of a representation of a gate tells a motorist about an approaching level crossing. But, what common sense would have us say is that while we indeed acquire *some* knowledge about the world from what we are only told (by one means or another), this is to be *contrasted* with the knowledge we acquire by *finding out for ourselves*, in short the knowledge we acquire by 'direct observation'. A motorist, for example, can *also* learn of a level crossing through actually observing it for himself (and he is *not* said to 'observe' it merely by interpreting a road sign in terms of it). If, therefore, I am to fulfil the task of uniting realism with common sense, I must somehow show that what common sense is here saying does not contradict anything I myself am saying. I must undertake, that is, to formulate a convincing analysis, within the framework of my account given so far, of what the contrast which common sense is here making really amounts to.

In order to place myself in a position where I can do this, I must first analyze in greater detail than has so far been possible the way in which visual and tactual sense-data perform their symbolic function.

[1] P. 62.

*

I have said that thanks to the process of evolution, we possess the innate capacity to interpret our visual and tactual sense-data in accordance with the conventions by which they are governed. There may or may not be a period in which the new-born infant experiences sense-data without thereby becoming apprised of his environment;[1] but anyway, he begins in due course *automatically* to interpret his visual and tactual sense-data correctly in terms of physical objects.

In saying this, however, I do not mean to imply that he goes through any *conscious process* of interpretation. On the contrary—and this is of paramount importance—he is wholly unaware that the objects of which he becomes conscious are made known to him by means of symbols. For he is not in any degree conscious of his visual and tactual sense-data as being anything different from the objects in terms of which he automatically interprets them. What this means is that if, say, some object is visually 'presented' to him by a red sense-datum, then he is conscious merely of a *red object*, and not of anything else in addition. He is not, that is to say, conscious at all of a red *colour-patch in his visual field as such*.

All this may seem, at first, somewhat extraordinary. But I think that it will seem less so if we reflect further. Let us consider the several paradoxes it may appear to involve one by one.

To begin with, it will surely be conceded that there is nothing odd about the notion of interpreting a symbol in terms of what it symbolizes without any conscious process of interpretation. When an accomplished motorist sees a specimen of the sign consisting of a representation of a gate, he does not consciously think to himself: 'The Ministry of Transport has laid down the convention that any placard by the side of the road bearing a representation of a gate is to symbolize the approach of a level crossing. Therefore, since the placard by the side of the road *here* contains this sign, it is serving to inform me that a level crossing lies ahead'. Nor, very likely, does he go through any conscious process whatever of *inferring* the existence of the crossing from that of the sign. What happens is that on seeing the sign he succumbs instantaneously to the belief that there is a crossing ahead, and although his seeing

[1] See above, p. 82n.

the sign is of course the reason for his succumbing to this belief, it need not consciously occur to him that this is so. We should none the less not hesitate to say that he had interpreted a symbol in terms of what it symbolized. There is, therefore, nothing in the least unfamiliar about the idea of so interpreting a symbol without any conscious process of interpretation.

But of course, it remains true that a motorist would be unable to interpret road signs in the way he does had he not at some time *learnt* their respective meanings. Suppose, however, that thanks to the progress of scientific invention, the Ministry of Transport were to issue a certain pill; and that the effect of swallowing it was to bring about the very same modifications of the brain as those actually brought about by the combined learning processes of studying the Highway Code and gaining sufficient experience of actual motoring—that is, such modifications as to make possible the correct and instantaneous interpretation of road signs. This supposition, fanciful though it be, is certainly not unintelligible. It serves, therefore, to demonstrate that it is intelligible to speak of our interpreting a symbol in terms of what it symbolizes both instantaneously *and* without ever having learnt its meaning. It is therefore intelligible to say, as I do, that thanks to evolution our brains are *at birth* of such a structure that we are able, without any prior learning, instantaneously to interpret our visual and tactual sense-data correctly in terms of physical objects.

A further objection may be made. It may be pointed out that to speak of the 'correct' interpretation of a symbol implies that the way in which it is interpreted accords with its *true* meaning, that is to say with the convention or conventions by which it is *really* governed. But what is meant by describing certain conventions as those by which it is really governed—i.e. regardless of how anyone may at any time *wrongly* interpret it? The only possible answer, it may be urged, is that conventions can be said 'really' to govern a symbol only in so far as *some person or persons* have at some time or other and in some way or other actually *laid them down*. Thus what makes it true to say that a particular road sign is really governed by such-and-such conventions—whatever any inexperienced motorist may think to the contrary—is the fact that the Ministry of Transport has, by such actions as the issuing of a particular booklet, laid down these particular conventions. Likewise, what makes it true to say that a particular word in the English language is really governed by such-and-such conventions—however much an uneducated person may depart from them—is the fact that a sufficient number of literate English-speaking persons has laid down these particular conventions—not in this case by making any official pronouncements, but simply by gradually adopting, over a long period of time, particular linguistic habits of expression.

Now in saying that we interpret our visual and tactual sense-data 'correctly' in terms of physical objects, I am saying that the way in which we interpret them accords with the conventions by which they are really governed. But who is it who has actually laid down these conventions? The only possible answer is that the 'person' to have laid them down is Nature. But there is no such person as Nature. And this being so, it may be asked whether there can be any conventions describable as those that really govern the sense-datum language. And this amounts to asking whether there can be any such *language* as the sense-datum language. For there can be no language without conventions that really govern it.

My answer to this objection is as follows. Although there is not literally such a person as Nature, this does not prevent many statements in which she is personified from being true. In particular, we constantly find her personified in statements widely believed to be true concerning evolutionary processes. Thus the possession by a certain species of a certain skill or other endowment may be explained by a biologist in a statement of such a form as: '*Nature has contrived that* members of this species possess . . . in order that they may be able to . . . and hence have higher prospects of living longer'. Such a statement involves the personification of Nature to the extent that she is credited (a) with contriving to bring about a particular end and (b) with doing this for a particular purpose. However, this way of talking has, on account of its neatness and succinctness, become so common and so universally accepted that statements of this kind need no qualification like 'so to speak' or 'if I may so put it'.

Now of course, it would be *possible* for the biologist to dispense entirely with all statements which thus involve the personification of Nature. This could be achieved by a lengthy reference, in every single statement describing some result of evolution, to the actual causal process whereby this result has come about. Likewise, it would be possible for me to state my account of perception without bringing in any mention of the sense-datum 'language'. I should begin by giving a laborious account of the causal process whereby the brain and sense-organs have come to be evolved, over a long period, in such a way that the human race today is able, through undergoing the perceptual experiences that it does, to acquire detailed knowledge about its physical environment. Having thus described the process whereby we have come to be able to have these experiences, I should then go on to state what our having them involves in a way which made no reference to this process. I might still find it convenient to speak of our 'interpreting' sense-data in accordance with certain *principles*— meaning thereby that the particular kinds of physical objects of which we become aware are *systematically dependent on* the particular kinds of sense-data which *make* us aware of them. What I should not speak of is our interpreting sense-data in accordance with 'linguistic conventions'. (As for analyzing the precise *way in which* our sense-data serve to make us aware of physical objects— to 'present' them to our consciousness—this is something which I am in any case about to do.)

However, granted that the personification of Nature is an established semantic device for the description of evolutionary processes, it seems to me overwhelmingly apposite, and at the same time illuminating, that my view of the evolutionary process whereby we have become able to acquire detailed knowledge of the physical world should be described in the way that I have in actual fact described it: by saying that in order to enable us to acquire such knowledge, Nature has devised a language—composed, as any language must be, of particular symbols governed by particular conventions—by means of which facts about this world may be communicated to us; and has, moreover, contrived that we are born with the innate capacity to understand this language. And inasmuch as it is Nature who has devised this language, it is Nature who has laid down the conventions governing its symbols. And because the evolutionary process in question can be described in this manner without any apology, we can on that account speak without apology of the 'correct interpretation' of sense-data.

I conclude that it is wholly intelligible to say that we interpret our visual and tactual sense-data correctly in terms of physical objects without any prior learning and without any conscious process of interpretation.

Given that we do this, is there anything at all surprising in the fact that we never, unless we start to philosophize, become conscious of our visual and tactual sense-data as anything distinct from the physical objects in terms of which we automatically interpret them? The idea of our interpreting the symbols of a language without ever being conscious of them as anything distinct from what they symbolize may seem at first a strange one. But it serves merely to emphasize the uniqueness of the sense-datum language and our mode of understanding it, a uniqueness which sets it apart from all man-made languages. It is true of any man-made language whatever that anyone who understands it is habitually conscious of its symbols as such, and hence as being something different from that which they symbolize. That the same does not apply in the case of (visual and tactual) sense-data is quite easy to grasp if we examine the unique features of the sense-datum language.

First, there is the very fact that our ability to understand this language requires no prior learning; whereas, on the other hand, we cannot understand any man-made language without first undergoing a process, often wearisome, of gradually bringing ourselves to associate the things constituting its symbols with whatever it is they symbolize. Often, we need to make a large conscious *effort* to force the relevant associations indelibly into our minds. In these circumstances, it is quite inevitable that we should be more than conscious of such symbols as something distinct from that which they symbolize. Not so with the symbols of the sense-datum language. Since we possess the innate capacity to associate visual and tactual sense-data of particular kinds with physical objects of particular kinds, there is no occasion on which their distinctness from one another is inescapably *forced on our attention*—as it would be by any conscious process of learning to associate the one with the other.

Furthermore, in the case of any man-made language, anyone who understands it must *once*, namely before he began to learn the language, have been confronted with the class of things constituting its symbols without in any way associating them with what they symbolize in the language. He will thus have indelibly implanted in him a full consciousness of such things *in their intrinsic nature*, so that when they eventually come to serve for him as symbols of something else, he will none the less clearly distinguish them from that which they symbolize. By contrast, we interpret our sense-data in terms of physical objects if not from the very moment we are born, at any rate soon afterwards; and if a period exists immediately after birth when we experience uninterpreted sense-data, this will certainly leave no indelible mark on our memories.

There is a third, no less important consideration. Our sense-data constitute the *sole* means whereby we are able to acquire knowledge about the class of objects—physical objects—whose existence they serve to symbolize. The case is quite different with the symbols of any man-made language. Thus *one* way in which we can ascertain that there is a table next door is by hearing someone utter words to this effect. But it is not the only way; for we can ascertain this also by actually seeing the table. Similarly, seeing the appropriate road sign is one but not the only way in which we can ascertain the existence of a level crossing. For we can ascertain this also by seeing instead the crossing itself. Now if, notwithstanding that certain symbols afford one means whereby we can ascertain the existence of certain objects, we none the less can also ascertain this by a more direct means in the absence of any such symbol, it would be odd indeed if when such a symbol *is* present to us we were not conscious of it as something distinct from the object whose existence it symbolizes. Thus again, the distinctness of the one from the other is forced on our attention.

There is, by contrast, no possibility of the distinctness of sense-data from physical objects being forced on our attention by this means, inasmuch as we never become apprised of physical objects in the absence of any sense-data.[1]

I contend that if we bear these three considerations in mind, there is nothing surprising in the fact that only a philosopher is ever conscious of the symbols of the sense-datum language as anything distinct from that which they symbolize.

We are now in a position to comprehend the remarkable 'vividness' with which sense-data 'present' physical objects to our consciousness—such that it is very much *as though* they had actually become part of our experience. I have mentioned already, in Sections II and III,[2] that this applies particularly to visual sense-data; and I shall, therefore, first discuss these separately before resuming any further mention of tactual sense-data.

The fact that we seem, in visual perception, to be 'directly experiencing' a physical object is not in the least perplexing once we have fully understood and accepted (a) that of course we really do 'directly experience' the visual sense-datum, it really is a feature of our experience, and (b) that we are, for the reasons just given, totally unconscious of this as being anything different from the physical object in terms of which we automatically and instantaneously interpret it. These two facts, moreover, besides enabling us to understand *why* we are visually conscious of physical objects in the way we are,[3] enable us also to understand

---

[1] But, it may be pointed out, while we indeed never become apprised of physical objects in the absence of any sense-data whatever, we do on occasion become apprised of them in the absence of any *visual or tactual* sense-data, i.e. through experiencing only sense-data belonging to the other senses. How, therefore, does this explain why we fail to differentiate physical objects specifically from visual and tactual sense-data (which alone constitute the symbols of the sense-datum language)? The only answer, I agree, is that it does not. It explains, if anything, why we fail to differentiate physical objects from sense-data *in general*—which raises the question whether this is actually the case. I shall argue later (pp. 100-4) that it is the case (albeit with a number of qualifications); and therefore I may include any explanation of *this* among my explanations of our failure to differentiate physical objects from visual and tactual sense-data.

[2] See pp. 51-2 and p. 68.

[3] Or rather why we are *conscious* of them *at all*, and do not merely *infer* their presence from our visual sense-data.

the precise *way in which* our consciousness of them thus 'simulates' our being conscious of features of our experience. They do this in the following way.[1]

Notwithstanding that we are in general not conscious of our visual sense-data, that is the contents of our visual field, *as such*, there are certain special and unusual cases in which we are—as when, for instance, we are induced in the psychological laboratory to experience an after-image, which is clearly distinguished in our consciousness from any physical object.[2] Again, it is said that a painter, on directing his eyes towards the objects around him, may be aware on occasion merely of a particular pattern of colours. Now, when we are visually conscious of a physical object, our mode of consciousness of this is very *like* our mode of consciousness of a visual sense-datum as such on those rare occasions when we have such consciousness. Even though a physical object is not, while a visual sense-datum is, a feature of our experience, nevertheless our consciousness of the former has the same *feel* as does our consciousness of the latter. Both have the same feel inasmuch as both have the feel of being a completely 'direct' or 'immediate' consciousness. In other words, even though our consciousness of the object actually involves, as our consciousness of the sense-datum does not, what I may call an 'informational medium', it does not *feel as though* our consciousness of *either* involves any such. To that extent, therefore, the experience of being visually conscious of a physical object has an all-important characteristic which it shares with such an experience as being conscious of an after-image; and it is to this characteristic that I am referring when I say that the former experience *seems* to involve the 'direct experiencing' of a physical object.

If the explanation which I have just given of this fact is to be fully understood, there is one further point which needs to be discussed. I have stated that the ordinary percipient is not conscious of his visual sense-data as anything distinct from the physical objects in terms of which he automatically interprets

---

[1] Compare Professor H. H. Price's remarks on what he calls the 'pseudo-intuitive' character of perceptual consciousness (*Perception*, pp. 150–69).

[2] I discuss this case below (p. 97).

them. He is not, that is to say, conscious of his visual sense-data as features of his experience. But how, it may be asked, is it possible to be conscious of something except *as* what it is? How is it possible to be conscious of a feature of our experience except *as* a feature of our experience, and hence as something distinct from any physical object?

The answer to this question is really perfectly simple. Consider our visual field. It consists, solely and simply, of *colours,* arranged in a particular pattern—the word 'colour' being here construed in a wide enough manner to include black and white. Now it can most certainly be said that we are conscious, in visual perception, of colours, and of colours *as such.* The point, however, is this: that when we are visually conscious of a physical object, while it is equally true that we are conscious of a physical object as such *and* that we are conscious of a pattern of colours as such, we are not conscious of these as two separate things. For in the experience of being visually conscious of a physical object, the pattern of colours becomes, so to speak, *affixed* in our consciousness to the physical object, so that we are seemingly conscious not of two things, but of a single thing, viz. *a coloured physical object.* With this in mind, the answer to the question 'How can we be conscious of a feature of our experience except *as* a feature of our experience?' is as follows. Where a thing answers to two descriptions, it is perfectly possible to be conscious of it *as* answering to one of them while not being conscious of it *as* answering to the other of them. Thus a savage who sees a clock for the first time may be conscious of it as a round object but not conscious of it as a clock. Similarly, when anyone at all is visually conscious of any physical object, he is conscious of a feature of his experience in the sense that he is conscious of what is in fact a feature of his experience, but he is conscious of it only as answering to some description other than that of being a feature of his experience—viz. the description of being a pattern of colours.[1]

---

[1] There is of course one important difference between the savage who is conscious of a round object but not of a clock and the visual percipient in general who is conscious of a colour but not of a feature of his experience—namely that not every round object of which a person is conscious is in fact a clock, whereas every

The matter may be put thus. Since, for the reasons I have given, the ordinary percipient does not differentiate his visual sense-data from the physical objects they 'present', he is conscious of them not as something *separate* from these objects—viz. features of his experience—but rather as *qualifying* them in a certain way, namely by constituting *the ways they look*, i.e. what he calls their 'visual appearances'. At the same time, he is not conscious of them as *mere* appearances; rather, inasmuch as he fails to differentiate visual sense-data from physical objects, so he fails to differentiate between the visual appearance of an object and the object itself. And thus he feels himself to be ('directly') *experiencing* the object and not merely its appearance. Most of us are, indeed, capable of isolating the visual appearance of an object in our minds for the purpose, say, of painting the object; and this is a practice which the professional painter cultivates to a fine art. But not only does achieving this require a considerable voluntary effort; even when it *is* achieved, we still do not, unless we happen to be philosophers, think of the appearance and the object itself as two separate things. Instead we think of the appearance as being an integral part of the object. For this reason, we ascribe to the object not only those properties, such as properties of shape, which belong both to the appearance *and* to the object itself, but also those properties, viz. properties of colour, which actually belong purely to the appearance.[1] And so we come to say not just that the object *looks* a certain colour but that it *is* that colour.

While, however, we do not in general distinguish between the visual appearance of an object and the object itself, there are nevertheless certain special occasions on which we do—namely those on which we happen to know that an object we see differs

colour of which a person is conscious *must* be a feature of his experience. Where, therefore, the savage is lacking in *factual information*, the visual percipient in general is lacking merely in *philosophical acumen*. Nevertheless, the analogy of the savage has a certain aptness: most of us are conscious of our visual sense-data, but not conscious of them *as* features of our experience, for the reason that most of us are philosophical savages.

[1] The question whether this involves an error, whether we can be said to be *mistaken* in ascribing colour to the object itself, was discussed in Section III (pp. 71–2).

in the way it looks from the way it is. As I have said previously,[1] we think of an object's appearance as on occasion differing from the object itself even in respect of colour, notwithstanding that the object itself is not ('intrinsically') coloured at all. Let us consider this case first.

I said, it will be remembered, that because in certain unusual conditions of observation an object looks a different colour from what it generally does, and because we know that the only reason for its so doing is the presence of these conditions rather than any change in the object itself, we are forced to say that in such conditions the colour it looks is different from the colour it *is*. Now it might be thought that by thus differentiating between its 'apparent' colour—i.e. the colour of which we are actually conscious—and its so-called 'real' colour, we must thereby become conscious of the former as something *distinct* from the object, and therefore be conscious of it *as* a feature of our experience. Thus, to take a very obvious example, if we look at an object through red spectacles, and thus become conscious of the colour red while being fully aware that the object is not 'really' red (but appears so *only* because we are wearing these spectacles), it is tempting to suppose that we must be conscious of this colour as being a mere feature of our experience. But I think that this supposition would be mistaken.

The plain fact is that despite our knowing that the colour red is not the 'real' colour of the object, this colour is none the less 'affixed' to the object in our consciousness just as much as would be the 'real' colour, so that we are still not conscious of the colour and the object as two separate things. We are, even in this case, seemingly conscious of one single thing, viz. *a physical object which looks red*. That is to say, we still regard the coloured sense-datum as qualifying the physical object it 'presents', and still by constituting its appearance, only *this* time its *mere* appearance. Admittedly, even many non-philosophers of sufficient intelligence would readily agree, if asked to reflect on this matter, that if we are conscious of a physical object which looks but is not 'really' red, then there must be something *other than* the physical object

[1] Section III, p. 69n.

which *is* red, viz. a colour-patch in our visual field. This has been considered sufficiently obvious to constitute the starting-point of the 'argument from illusion'. But it is not something that ever occurs to us unless we bring our reflective intellect to bear on the matter; and most of us never do so. It is simply false to say that an ordinary percipient who is conscious of a physical object which looks red, but which he knows to be 'really' some other colour, is conscious of the physical object and the colour red as two separate things. His experience is just not *like that*.

Contrast it with a very special, out-of-the-ordinary case where we *are* conscious of a physical object and a colour as two separate things, viz. the situation where we are induced in the psychological laboratory to experience an after-image. Suppose that, as the result of having carried out the appropriate instructions, we see a red circle 'on' a wall which we know to be 'really' white all over. In these circumstances, the nature of our experience is such that we are very definitely clearly conscious of two separate things, viz. (i) the wall, a physical object, and (ii) the after-image, a feature of our experience. The red circle does *not* become 'affixed' to the wall in such a way that we are conscious merely of a (white) wall *which looks red at one point*. The red circle is something as much distinct, in our consciousness, from the wall as would be a piece of red paper stuck on it. Only of course we happen to know that the red circle is not, like a piece of red paper, a physical object.

The exceptional character of this case is immediately apparent. Whereas the sitter in the psychological laboratory would not hesitate to say that he was conscious both of a wall and also of a red colour-patch, the wearer of red spectacles who is gazing un-reflectingly at what he knows to be 'really' a white wall would be most unlikely to describe his experience in this fashion. If asked what he is visually aware of, he would reply simply 'A wall which looks red'.

The same point applies to those circumstances in which we know that the *shape* an object looks is different from the shape it is—this difference being one which really is constituted by a discrepancy between the character of the object's appearance and the ('intrinsic') character of the object itself. Thus, we should not expect a person who was looking at a straight stick partly in water —which therefore looked bent—to say that he was conscious both of a stick partly in water and also of a V-shaped colour-patch. Once again, the fact constituting the first step in the 'argument from illusion' simply never occurs to the ordinary person.

It would be inaccurate to say that he is conscious of an item in his visual field as such even in the case of a complete hallucination which he suffers in the knowledge that it is one. Suppose a D.T.s sufferer 'sees' a pink rat and is alive to the fact that it is unreal. It would probably not occur to him that *part* of what he is conscious of *is* real, viz. the colour pink. This would be inseparable in his consciousness from the rat. So that if asked what he is visually aware of, he would make no mention of his visual field but would reply simply 'A pink rat, which, however, I know to be a figment of my imagination'.

Similarly with more humdrum, everyday 'illusions' of vision. For instance, when a person sees his image in a mirror, he knows that his body is not actually located behind the mirror. But if asked what he is visually aware of, he will make no reference in his reply to the contents of his visual field. Rather he will say, for example, that what he is visually aware of is his body 'looking as though it were' a short distance behind the mirror. Likewise, when a person looks up at the sky, he does not believe that the blue 'vault of Heaven' which meets his eyes really exists 'up there'. But his attention is not drawn on that account to the contents of his visual field.

In short, the non-philosopher, the 'plain man', is very, very rarely conscious of his visual field, that is of his visual sense-data, as such. He is conscious of them only as being what he calls the 'visual appearances' of physical objects. At the same time, in failing to differentiate visual sense-data from the physical objects they 'present', he is not—in general—conscious of a distinction between the visual appearance of an object and the object itself—with the result that he *seems* to be 'directly experiencing' the object. And even in cases where he is aware that an object's visual appearance is different in character from the object itself, he is still not conscious of the former as an entirely separate entity. For he still thinks of it as qualifying the object, only this time as its *mere* appearance.

Just as he is not in general conscious of his visual sense-data as such, so too he is not in general conscious of his tactual sense-data as such. That is to say, he is conscious of them not as something separate from the physical objects in terms of which he automatically interprets them, but again as qualifying them, in this case by constituting their *tactual* 'appearances', i.e. the ways they feel. And he is, again, not (usually) conscious of them as mere appearances, but as being an integral part of the objects themselves. Thus if, on touching a certain object, he experiences a warm sensation of touch, then he is tactually conscious not of two things, both this object and this sensation, but of a single thing, namely a warm object.[1]

I should say, however, that he does not think of the way a physical object feels as being quite as *much* an integral part of the object itself as is the way it looks. For if he touches an object with his eyes closed, although he does not feel himself to be ('directly') experiencing *only* its tactual appearance, he nevertheless does not feel himself either to be experiencing the object itself to quite the same *degree* as he would were he seeing it (even were he seeing and *not* touching it).[2] It would probably be comparatively easy to persuade almost anyone that an object he touches and the sensation of touch it induces in him are two separate things. In short (as I have remarked previously), tactual sense-data do not 'present'

---

[1] This is not entirely correct; for he very possibly *may* be tactually conscious of two things, viz. (i) the warm object he is touching and (ii) some warm part of his *own body*, namely that part of it (e.g. his hand) with which he is touching this object. The tactual sense-datum, therefore, serves to 'present' two different physical objects. But he is still not conscious of it as something distinct from either of them; that is to say, he is tactually conscious of two (warm) physical objects, but not of two physical objects *plus* a feature of his experience.

[2] This remains true, in my opinion, even though we regard the sense of touch as a more *trustworthy* source of information about the physical world on account of the fact that tactual 'illusions' are far rarer than visual ones. This fact has led some philosophers to suppose, quite wrongly, that touch actually affords us a uniquely 'direct' awareness of physical objects, and even that it provides *conclusive proof* of their existence.

physical objects with a degree of 'vividness' entirely comparable to that with which visual sense-data do.

How, then, are we to explain this difference?[1] I would draw attention for this purpose to the following consideration. On the one hand, our visual sense-data supply us with their information about physical objects with a truly remarkable speed and precision. Compare them in this respect with the words of a man-made language. It is plain enough that we can learn far more about the exact shapes, sizes and spatial relations of the objects in a room by looking at them—even by only glancing at them for an instant—than we could from a description of them, however minute and prolonged, by someone else. On the other hand, our tactual sense-data do not 'present' physical objects to us with anything like the same speed or precision. We cannot begin to learn the exact shape even of a single object by touch alone without laboriously and time-consumingly feeling our way all over its surface; and even when this operation is completed, we shall still not expect to be *as* fully informed about it as we should have been by a visual examination. Given, now, that our visual and tactual sense-data both serve in some degree to give the impression of our being in 'direct contact' with the physical world, it is only to be expected that this impression would be all the more striking in the case of visual sense-data on account of their higher speed and precision in 'presenting' physical objects.[2]

As regards sense-data other than visual and tactual ones, we do not have the innate capacity to interpret these in terms of physical objects, but come to associate them with physical objects of particular kinds through experience alone. For this reason, I have not found it appropriate to speak of them as 'symbols' governed by 'linguistic conventions' laid down by Nature. When, therefore,

---

[1] It may be due partly to the very fact that a single tactual sense-datum frequently 'presents' two physical objects, that touched and that touching: it is perhaps less easy on this account to fail *altogether* to differentiate it from one of them alone. But I think that this is not the only or even the main reason.

[2] This explains a point which I made early on in the very first section (p. 25), namely that the dichotomy between perceptual experiences and perceived physical objects is initially harder to swallow (even for a philosopher) in the realm of sight than in that of touch.

I originally asked, 'Why are we not conscious of the symbols of the sense-datum language as anything distinct from that which they symbolize?', I endeavoured to explain this fact by reference to certain differences between visual and tactual sense-data and the symbols of any man-made language:[1] I did not, in this context, examine at all sense-data of other kinds. The question arises however: are those particular considerations whereby I explained our failure to differentiate visual and tactual sense-data from physical objects such as hold equally good for *all* sense-data? Were it to turn out that they are, and were it at the same time *not* to turn out that we fail to differentiate all sense-data alike from physical objects, then I should be proved wrong in taking these particular considerations to supply the explanation, or at least the whole explanation, for our failure so to differentiate visual and tactual sense-data. But this is not what turns out. On the contrary, if we briefly re-examine these considerations and then examine independently the extent to which we so differentiate *auditory*, *olfactory and gustatory* sense-data, we shall find that the latter accords perfectly with what the former would lead us to expect. Let us therefore first re-examine these considerations one by one and see how far, if at all, they hold good for all sense-data and not just for visual and tactual ones.

First, I cited the fact[2] that whereas we have the innate capacity to interpret visual and tactual sense-data in terms of physical objects, in the case of a man-made language we have to undergo a conscious process of gradually *learning* to associate the things constituting its symbols with whatever it is they symbolize. As the result, the distinctness of symbols from that which they symbolize is forced on our attention in the latter case, as it is not in the former.

It appears at first glance that this point applies only to visual and tactual sense-data, since we do associate our other sense-data with physical objects of particular kinds only by learning how to do so. However, I think that while we do not have the capacity to acquire these latter associations without the relevant *experience*, we do have the capacity to acquire them—given this experience—

[1] See pp. 90–2.   [2] Pp. 90–1.

without any *conscious effort*. Thus in general, once physical objects of certain kinds are found to produce a certain sound, smell or taste, then that sound, smell or taste alone comes in future *automatically* to be associated with objects of those kinds. While, therefore, this association is learned, in the sense that it is acquired only through experience, it is not *consciously* learned at all. Not so the associations acquired by us in the course of learning a man-made language: even the child who first learns to understand his native tongue does not do so without *any* conscious effort. It can be said therefore that, unlike our associations of man-made symbols with whatever they symbolize, our associations of *all* sense-data with physical objects of particular kinds are acquired without any conscious learning process. And an *unconscious* learning process in the case of sense-data other than visual and tactual ones is not, I think, sufficient to force on our attention their distinctness from physical objects. I conclude, therefore, that as regards this first of my explanations for our failure to differentiate visual and tactual sense-data from physical objects, it holds equally good for all sense-data. But this is not true of my second explanation.

'In the case', I said,[1] 'of any man-made language, anyone who understands it must *once*, namely before he began to learn the language, have been confronted with the class of things constituting its symbols without in any way associating them with what they symbolize in the language. He will thus have indelibly implanted in him a full consciousness of such things *in their intrinsic nature*, so that when they eventually come to serve for him as symbols of something else, he will none the less clearly distinguish them from that which they symbolize. By contrast, we interpret our sense-data in terms of physical objects if not from the very moment we are born, at any rate soon afterwards; and if a period exists immediately after birth when we experience uninterpreted sense-data, this will certainly leave no indelible mark on our memories.'

Now it is reasonable to assume that as soon as a child interprets visual and tactual sense-data for the first time, he begins *im-*

[1] P. 91.

mediately to acquire associations between particular sounds, smells and tastes and physical objects of particular kinds. That is to say, such sounds, smells and tastes alone come immediately to serve for him as 'signs' of the presence of such objects. And therefore the fact that he *once* experienced these without having acquired this association will leave no more of a mark on his memory than the fact that he may also have experienced uninterpreted visual and tactual sense-data. As far as this goes, therefore, there is no unique inducement to his differentiating auditory, olfactory and gustatory sense-data from physical objects. However, throughout the entire course of his life he is likely on occasion to encounter some sound, smell or taste which he has not encountered before, and where he has no means of knowing what is producing it he will be unable to associate it with any kind of physical object. This, therefore, will serve permanently to instil in him a full consciousness of its intrinsic nature, so that even if he subsequently does come to associate it with a physical object of some kind, he will clearly distinguish between the two. But not only this; if he distinguishes some *particular* sounds, smells or tastes from the physical objects which produce them, he can scarcely avoid so distinguishing sounds, smells or tastes *in general*: that all such are generically the same can scarcely elude his notice.

As for my final point[1]—namely that we never become apprised of physical objects in the absence of sense-data—I noted at the time that this explains, if anything, why we fail to differentiate sense-data *in general* from physical objects.

I conclude, therefore, that of these three considerations the first and third hold equally good for all sense-data, while the second, on the other hand, actually suggests that we *should* thus differentiate auditory, olfactory and gustatory sense-data.

If we now ask how far we do this, we find that the answer accords perfectly with this conclusion. We do not differentiate them entirely—as we should expect from considerations 1 and 3; but we none the less do so up to a point—as we should equally expect from consideration 2. On the one hand, as with visual and tactual sense-data, we regard auditory, olfactory and gustatory

[1] Pp. 91–2.

sense-data not as something separate from physical objects—as mere 'private' sensations—but as qualifying them, this time by constituting the ways they sound, smell or taste. On the other hand, by contrast with visual and tactual sense-data, we regard them in *all* cases as *mere* 'appearances'. That is, we do not regard an object's sound, smell or taste, as we do its visual or tactual appearance, as an integral part of it: in only hearing, smelling or tasting some object, we do not feel ourselves to be 'directly experiencing' the object itself at all. And this explains a fact which has puzzled some philosophers, namely that we commonly speak of *inferring* an object's presence from its sound or smell, whereas we do not speak of inferring this from the sight or feel of it.

I am now in a position to answer the objection to my whole account of perception that I stated above.[1] The objection came to this: that our sense-data merely *tell us* about the physical world much as a road sign tells a motorist about a level crossing; and therefore we can no more be said to 'observe' physical objects than a motorist can be said to 'observe' a crossing merely by interpreting a road sign in terms of it.

While it is said that my account makes physical objects unobservable, it will be agreed at least that it does not make unobservable such things as after-images. Inasmuch as we are seldom conscious of items in our visual field as such, we seldom have occasion to talk of 'observing' things of this sort. But when we do talk of this, there is no possible reason why we ought not to. For our consciousness of things which are themselves features of our experience plainly does *not* involve any 'informational medium'.

So at least the observability of after-images is left unscathed by my account. The point, however, is this: that although our consciousness of physical objects *does* involve an 'informational medium'—and must do so, since we cannot 'directly experience' them—nevertheless the way we are conscious of these, at least in visual perception, is just *like* the way we are conscious (if ever we are) of items in our visual field as such. As I noted above,[2] it does

[1] P. 85.   [2] P. 93.

not *feel as though* our consciousness of the former is in any degree less 'direct' than our consciousness of the latter. That is, it does not feel as though our consciousness of *either* involves any 'informational medium'.

This being so, it is very natural that we should use *one and the same set of verbs* to describe our consciousness both of our visual field as such and of visually 'presented' physical objects; and further, that we should use these to *contrast* such consciousness with finding out about things 'indirectly' or at second hand. Thus we talk of 'seeing' both after-images and physical objects of which we are visually conscious. On the other hand, we do not say that a motorist 'sees' a level crossing if he learns of it only from a road sign. For he is not then *conscious of* the crossing at all, let alone in the same manner as that in which either someone is conscious of an after-image or he himself is conscious of the sign. Accordingly, we say that the sign, which alone he *sees*, merely *tells* him about the crossing.

And so it is too with the word 'observe'. We 'observe' both after-images and physical objects of which we are visually conscious; but a motorist does not 'observe' a crossing in learning of it only from a sign. 'Observe', unlike 'see', is not confined in its use to the field of *visual* consciousness. We can be said, for example, to 'observe' sounds and smells, and in general anything of which we either are or seem to be 'directly conscious'. It is significant, however, that we do not naturally talk of 'observing' *physical objects* by any of the senses other than sight. We hardly 'observe' the objects in a pitch-dark room which we can feel but not see. And to talk of 'observing' objects by sound, smell or taste alone would be artificial in the extreme. No one, on entering a room which emitted a smell of onions (these being concealed from view), would exclaim that he observed onions; but only that he observed the smell of onions.[1] The reason for this is apparent after what has been said. In merely smelling an object, we are barely conscious of the object itself at all, and may actually talk of

[1] He might say he observed *that* there were onions in the room. But observing *that something is the case* is a very different matter from observing something—just as seeing that something is the case is from seeing something.

'inferring' its presence.[1] And even touch, while affording us some consciousness of physical objects, is not, for reasons I have given,[2] comparable in this respect to sight. Visual sense-data stand alone in the 'vividness' with which they 'present' physical objects. Only they serve fully to give us the impression of 'directly experiencing' the physical world.

I conclude that my account of perception does *not* make physical objects unobservable. To suppose that it does is to misinterpret our use of the word 'observe'. The ordinary person, in saying that he has 'observed' some object, is not expressing a philosophical theory as to the nature of his 'contact' with the physical world. All he is saying, and all he either knows or cares about, is that he learned of this object's existence through being *conscious of it*, and *without* being conscious of anything in the nature of an 'informational medium'. Whether there really *was* any such medium is a question only a philosopher would raise.

I claim, therefore, to have healed the breach, in the way I promised above,[3] between 'realism' and common sense. That is, I have given, within the terms of my account of perception, what seems to me a convincing analysis of our ordinary distinction between first and second hand knowledge about the world.

Before developing my account further, I should like at this point to examine two other objections frequently brought against any realist account of the physical world.

The first of these invokes the Humean principle that we could never form the *conception* of a set of objects entirely distinct from anything of which we have had 'immediate experience'. I call this principle 'Humean' since it is a direct offshoot of Hume's principle that all our 'ideas' are derived from previously experienced 'impressions'. Accordingly, let us begin by examining the grounds on which Hume subscribed to this principle.[4]

The word 'impression' is used by him to denote what he calls our 'sensations, passions, and emotions'; however, the illustrations

---

[1] See above, p. 104.   [2] Pp. 99–100.   [3] P. 85.
[4] *Vide* David Hume, *A Treatise of Human Nature*, Book I, Part I, section i.

which he gives in this connection and which I shall discuss are all
drawn from sensations, and we may equate what he calls 'sensations' with what we call 'sense-data'. As for his use of the word
'idea', I intend to discuss this at some length, since I believe that
everything hinges upon it. Putting it aside for a moment—he
establishes the principle of the dependency of our 'ideas' on our
'impressions' by a simple process of observation and induction.
He examines a large quantity of his 'ideas' and finds that he can
trace all of them to 'impressions' which he has previously experienced. Having further observed that *anyone's* range of 'ideas' is
apparently limited by the range of his previously experienced
'impressions', he takes himself to have proved the general pro-
position that all 'ideas' are and can be derived only from such
'impressions'. And on the strength of this, he thereafter takes it for
granted that no one can have any conception of 'external' objects,
that is of objects 'specifically different from' all 'impressions'.

Let us now examine closely some of his statements.

'The first circumstance that strikes my eye,' he says, 'is the
great resemblance betwixt our impressions and ideas. . . . When
I shut my eyes and think of my chamber, the ideas I form are exact
representations of the impressions I felt; nor is there any circumstance of the one which is not to be found in the other.'

Clearly, the 'ideas' to which he is here referring are to be
equated with *images*, in this case visual images which 'represent'
his previously experienced visual 'impressions'. He himself, indeed, frequently describes 'ideas' as 'images' throughout. We
must therefore consider what it is to have an image.

To have an image is to *imagine* yourself having a sensory
experience of a kind that you are not in fact having. (The words
'imagine' and 'imagination' figure constantly in Hume's lines.) If
you are asked to conjure up an olfactory image 'of' a rose, what
you are being asked to do is to imagine yourself having the
olfactory experience that you normally have when you actually
smell a rose. Likewise, to have an auditory image 'of' a telephone
ringing is to imagine yourself having the auditory experience that
you normally have when you actually hear a telephone ringing.
And to have a visual image 'of' some particular kind of physical

object is to imagine yourself having the visual experience that you normally have when you actually see an object of that kind.

With this in mind, we can readily formulate the meaning intended to be conveyed in the following passage, which can be said to form the kernel of Hume's argument.

Having stated in general terms that he can find no instance of an 'idea' not derived from a previous 'impression', he then says: 'To confirm this, I consider another plain and convincing phaenomenon; which is, that wherever, by any accident, the faculties which give rise to any impressions are obstructed in their operations, as when one is born blind or deaf, not only the impressions are lost, but also their correspondent ideas; so that there never appear in the mind the least traces of either of them. Nor is this only true where the organs of sensation are entirely destroyed, but likewise where they have never been put in action to produce a particular impression. We cannot form to ourselves a just idea of the taste of a pine-apple without having actually tasted it'.

After what I have said, the considerations to which Hume is here directing our attention can now be stated in the following simple terms. Firstly, a man born blind who has never had any visual experiences cannot form visual images, that is, there is no kind of visual experience which he can even imagine himself having; and equally there is no kind of auditory experience which a man born deaf can imagine *himself* having. Secondly, a person's powers of imagery are limited by the limits of his past experience within the realm of any one of the senses. Thus one who in general is expert at forming all manner of gustatory images is powerless to imagine the taste of a pineapple if he has never actually tasted one. Likewise, one with an outstanding capacity for visual imagery cannot imagine a colour totally unlike any he has ever actually experienced. (I say 'totally unlike' because, as Hume goes on to say, he may well be able to imagine a *shade* of blue, for example, not corresponding precisely with any shade of blue he has ever actually experienced.)

We are now in a position to interpret Hume's conclusion that all 'ideas' are derived from previously experienced 'impressions'. What this comes to is that no one can ever imagine himself having a sensory experience entirely unlike any that he has ever actually had. This is not quite correct, since Hume uses the word 'impression' to cover what he calls our 'inner perceptions' (our feelings of emotion, desire, etc.) besides those that are 'conveyed by the senses'; and an 'idea' is a 'representation' of an 'impression' of any kind.[1] Accordingly, we must interpret his principle as stating that no one can imagine himself having *any* experience, sensory or otherwise, entirely unlike any that he has ever actually had.

Now, I have no quarrel whatever to pick with this principle. There is indeed ample evidence to support it. But it does not remotely follow that the notion of something distinct from all possible experiences is an incomprehensible one. For the question of whether we can understand this notion is a wholly *different* question from the question of what kinds of experiences we can and cannot imagine ourselves having; and in settling the latter question, Hume is not entitled to assume, as he does, that he has thereby also settled the former—this having nothing whatever to do with our powers of *imagery*.

It is indeed the case that there can be no 'idea' of an object distinct from all possible 'impressions'; for this is ruled out by the meaning which Hume attaches to the word 'idea'. He does, in fact, first *introduce* this word as denoting an 'image' of an 'impression' (though I have so far deliberately ignored this, what matters being how he actually uses the word in practice). But the question of what does and does not fall within our understanding cannot be settled simply by choosing to use a certain word in a certain way. Granted that our understanding, if we have any such, of the notion of an 'external' object is not to be described as an 'idea', we must find some other word for it: let us speak, as Hume himself does on occasion, of our 'conception' of such an object. The question, therefore, is whether, apart from our ability to form 'ideas'—that is to *imagine* particular kinds of 'impressions'—we can also form a 'conception' of something entirely different from

[1] Hume himself often uses the word 'image' in connection with all our 'ideas', though we should nowadays normally use this word to denote only the imagining of a *sensory* experience.

any 'impressions'. And this question is plainly not to be answered by observing what 'ideas' we do and do not have. Yet it is precisely by this means that Hume regards this question as having been answered; that is, having failed to observe any 'idea' not derived from a previous 'impression', and having concluded from this that there *can* be no such, he rejects forthwith as nonsensical 'the notion of external existence, when taken for something specifically different from our perceptions'.[1]

We may now begin to wonder how it is possible that Hume should have succumbed to what seems on the face of it such transparently fallacious reasoning. To understand this fully might require a minute and comprehensive discussion of his entire thought. But I shall suggest two reasons which may help to explain his seemingly perfunctory dismissal of 'the notion of external existence'.

First, there can scarcely be any doubt that he trades, albeit unconsciously, on the *ordinary* connotation of the word 'idea' according to which we have the 'idea' of any notion which we understand or think we understand. And it is all the more inevitable that he should have fallen into this trap in view of the fact that his predecessor Locke had himself introduced this word 'to stand for whatsoever is the object of the understanding when a man thinks'. That he does indeed fall into this trap is borne out by a number of his statements. For example, in discussing the question why we acquire the mistaken (as he thinks) belief that objects continue to exist 'when they are not present to the senses',[2] he allows himself to speak on one occasion of the 'idea of continued existence' notwithstanding that, mistaken or not, this is certainly *not* an 'idea' in his sense: no 'idea' can 'represent' an object as continuing to exist when we are no longer having any 'impression', since to form 'ideas' is precisely to imagine ourselves having certain 'impressions'. He does, it is true, switch abruptly in the very same sentence, as if to correct himself, to the word 'conception'. But if he is at least tempted to use the word 'idea' in connection with our common notions regarding the 'external' existence of objects,

[1] *A Treatise of Human Nature*, Book I, Part IV, section ii.
[2] Ibid.

then it is quite easy to see how he comes to reject these notions as fictitious. Having defined an 'idea' as an 'image' of an 'impression', he first establishes that all 'ideas' are derived from previous 'impressions' by a thorough examination of the scope and limits of our powers of imagery, in other words by an empirical survey of what really *are* 'ideas' in his sense. It is then only too easy for him to conclude that we have no (real) conception of something distinct from 'impressions' on the ground that if we did, this would involve a repudiation of his established principle concerning the 'origin' of all our 'ideas'. But of course it is only by initially *ignoring* the question whether we have such a conception —and justifiably in view of his original definition of 'idea'—that he has succeeded in establishing this principle.

The second point that I want to make is, perhaps, of more fundamental importance, since it provides a reason not only why Hume himself rejected 'external' objects, but also why *any* philosopher may be tempted to do so even if he avoids the pitfalls engendered by Hume's use of the word 'idea'.

The fact is that, in Hume's view, 'the unthinking and unphilosophical part of mankind' really do *not* form any notion, *even a fictitious one*, of objects 'specifically different from our perceptions', but rather 'suppose their perceptions to be their only objects, and never think of a double existence internal and external'.[1] He considered, in other words, that the ordinary person *equates* the objects he perceives with his 'perceptions', that is with his sensory 'impressions' or in short his sense-data. And this assumption, though in my view mistaken, is one which it is very easy for any philosopher to make. For although, in my view, we become aware in perception of objects distinct from all possible sense-data, we nevertheless fail to differentiate between these objects and the sense-data which *make* us aware of them; and therefore, given the two facts (a) that we experience sense-data and (b) that we do indeed 'never think of a double existence', it is easy to conclude that sense-data must constitute the sole objects of our perceptual awareness. In other words, because we are not conscious of sense-data as anything distinct from the physical

[1] Ibid.

objects in terms of which we automatically interpret them, a philosopher may easily fail to spot the fact that we have submitted them to any process of interpretation at all.

Hume, therefore, denied that we have a conception of objects distinct from 'impressions' not merely because this appeared to contradict the principle that all our 'ideas' are derived from previous 'impressions', but also on the basis of what he took to be the observed character of our perceptual experiences and our conception of objects to which these give rise. He regarded the notion of objects 'specifically different from our perceptions' as an invention not of mankind in general, but of *philosophers* who had misrepresented our ordinary beliefs as to what it is that we perceive. Accordingly, he conceived the question 'why we attribute a *continued* existence to objects, even when they are not present to the senses; and why we suppose them to have an existence *distinct* from the mind and perception' as the question why we attribute a continued and distinct existence to our (sensory) *impressions*. In other words, he believed not that we regard objects as existing independently of our sense-data, but that we regard our sense-data as existing independently of our experiencing them. And if this were really so, he would be entirely justified in taking it to involve a straight contradiction.

Hume's thought has had a profound influence on the entire course of modern philosophy. The doctrine of phenomenalism, according to which physical objects are not to be *equated* with sense-data but rather to be thought of as complex 'logical constructions' out of hypothetical as well as actual sense-data, can be regarded as a sophisticated version of Hume's own view—an attempt to reconcile it with common sense by allowing that there is a sense in which physical objects really do exist independently of our perceiving them. The phenomenalist fully accepts Hume's view that 'everything which appears to the mind is nothing but a perception', and that it is only certain misguided philosophers who have ever thought otherwise. Professor Ayer, for example, notes approvingly how Hume rejected 'the "philosophical" assumption that besides one's perceptions, which alone were directly given, there existed an independent set of objects' as involving 'an entirely unwarrantable re-duplication of the perceptual world'.[1]

I have suggested two separate reasons why Hume rejected this assumption. He did so partly because it appeared to contravene the observed facts as to the nature of our perceptual awareness, but partly also as the result of confused reasoning due to his none too precise use of the word 'idea'. Since, however, his modern followers have not on the whole taken over his use of this word, it is natural to assume that they are not themselves guilty of any such confusion, but owe their allegiance to him *only* to the extent that they believe he correctly represented the facts of perception.

But I think that this assumption would be over-charitable. For if it were just that we do not *perceive* a set of objects entirely distinct from our sense-data, the question would still remain open whether there might nevertheless not *be* such objects. But it is invariably held by phenomenalists not merely that such objects are unknown to us, but that the very suggestion of their existence is completely meaningless. And the reason this is held to be meaningless is that we could never (even) form the *conception* of a set of objects wholly distinct from anything of which we have had, or can imagine ourselves having, 'immediate experience'. And it is this principle which I described at the outset of this discussion as a direct offshoot of Hume's principle that all our 'ideas' are derived from previous 'impressions'. It can, indeed, be said to constitute the very essence of the doctrine of *empiricism*,[2] which has dominated twentieth-century philosophy and of which Hume is the acknowledged father. And it undoubtedly does provide one reason for embracing phenomenalism: it is held not only that our senses do not *in fact* supply us with knowledge (even indirect knowledge) of objects distinct from our sense-data, but also that it is *quite impossible that they should do so*, since the notion of such objects is entirely beyond our comprehension. Since those who

---

[1] A. J. Ayer, *The Foundations of Empirical Knowledge*, p. 243.

[2] I say it constitutes the 'essence' of empiricism since its acceptance is what chiefly *distinguishes* the empiricist from the non-empiricist philosopher. I myself, who perhaps can be said to depart from empiricism as much as anyone does at the present time, none the less, as I shall show in a moment, fully accept certain *other* principles commonly taken to be implied by the word 'empiricism'.

hold this constantly acknowledge their debt to Hume, it is reasonable to assume that they do so on the strength of his empirical observations as to the 'origin' of all our 'ideas', and of their own confirmation of these observations. But if it is indeed for this reason that they reject as senseless the 'realist' notion of physical objects, then the only possible comment I have to make is that this is an invalid reason, since, as I have shown, these observations were directed exclusively towards our powers of imagery and not towards our powers of understanding in general.

If, on the other hand, they reject this notion not on the strength of any empirical observations, but because they regard it as a self-evident *a priori* principle that *experience* ultimately constitutes the sole object of our understanding, then I can only reply: first, that Hume himself never so regarded either this or any other principle but relied for his conclusions entirely on observation, and secondly, that it does not at any rate appear to *me* self-evident. On the contrary, what I find much *more* self-evident is the falsity of a number of conclusions to which it leads.[1]

However, in case the reader should exaggerate the extremity of my anti-empiricist position and thereby attribute to me absurdities of which I am not guilty, let me say at once that there are certain principles, commonly dubbed 'empiricist', which I do accept and which I have not repudiated in my account of perception.

First, I accept the principle that all our factual knowledge is and must be derived from experience and observation, as distinct from *a priori* reasoning. I have never supposed that we acquire knowledge about the physical world in any way other than by having particular kinds of perceptual experiences. What I have rejected is the further assumption that this knowledge is not merely derived from but is ultimately knowledge *about* experience.[2]

Not only do I accept that experience is the source of all our

---

[1] That is, all the paradoxes (discussed in Section III) yielded by phenomenalism.

[2] This poses the question, which the phenomenalist would say is unanswerable, how experience can possibly supply us with genuine knowledge about something altogether different from any experience. This question is discussed in Section V.

(factual) *knowledge*. I should even agree that there is at any rate a clear sense in which it is the source of all our powers of understanding, our 'ideas' in the broadest sense. For I am content to go along with certain statements made by Locke on the question whether or not we have 'innate ideas'.[1]

'It is an established opinion among some men,' he says, 'that there are in the understanding certain innate principles; some primary notions, κοιναί ἔννοιαί, characters, as it were, stamped upon the mind of man, which the soul receives in its very first being, and brings into the world with it.' He goes on to denounce this opinion on the ground that 'our observation, employed either about external sensible objects, or about the internal operations of our minds, perceived and reflected on by ourselves, is that which supplies our understandings with all the materials of thinking'.

The point to which I would draw particular attention is that Locke denied the existence of 'innate ideas'—a fact commonly regarded as conferring on him the title of 'empiricist'—*even though* he took a 'realist' view of the nature of physical objects which largely coincides with my own. He held, as I do, that while such properties as colour and taste do not 'really exist in' physical objects (or as I have preferred to express it do not belong to them 'intrinsically'), nevertheless such properties as shape, size and motion do 'exist in' them, and to that extent physical objects are perceived by us as they are 'in themselves'.[2] Thus a moving object, he says, 'produces in us' the 'idea of motion' which 'represents it as it really is in' the object.[3] Our 'ideas', therefore, though themselves 'in us', nevertheless afford us an understanding of 'external' objects. In spite of this, Locke is anxious to make the point that this understanding first comes to be 'supplied' to us through our actually observing such objects; it is not 'stamped upon the mind of man' from the first. And with this I in no way disagree. For I

[1] *Vide* John Locke, *An Essay concerning Human Understanding*, Book I, ch. 2 and Book II, ch. 1.

[2] *Vide* ibid, Book II, ch. 8.

[3] He did not, in fact, take the same view as I do of *how* our 'ideas' (which in this context are to be equated with sense-data) 'represent' physical objects. He believed, as I do not (see above p. 81n.), that they do so by, and only by, (partially) *resembling* physical objects.

have never suggested, nor have I any reason for wanting to suggest, that a child goes through any process of 'forming a conception of' physical objects *before* he first comes to observe them through automatically interpreting his sense-data in terms of them —still less that he has this conception from the very first instant of his life.

But, it may be said, he would surely be unable so to interpret his sense-data unless he *already* understood what a physical object is. However, this would be correct only if he underwent, as he does not, a conscious process of interpretation. The fact is, rather, that his interpretation is instantaneous, and can be said to this extent not to consist in any *process* at all. I have no objection to saying that this interpretation *involves* his understanding what a physical object is, but this must not be taken to imply that such understanding *precedes* the interpretation.

It must not be taken to imply either that it is constituted by some concomitant mental activity *distinct from* the interpretation. If we are to say that being perceptually conscious of a physical object involves understanding the notion of a physical object, we must equally say that having an *image*, an 'idea' in Hume's sense, involves understanding the notion of an experience of the kind that is being imagined. But no one would suggest that whenever we form an image, we indulge in *two* separate activities, viz. (i) 'forming a conception of' the kind of experience in question and (ii) actually imagining ourselves having an experience of this kind.

When, therefore, a child observes a physical object for the first time, nothing whatever takes place in his mind *apart from* an awareness, as Locke says a purely *passive* awareness, of an object in his environment.[1] And there is nothing in the least mysterious or 'philosophical' about the notion of such awareness, since it is something entirely familiar and commonplace to us all. In putting forward my account of the nature of perceptual consciousness, I have sought to do nothing more than formulate what I take to be an accurate description of everyone's ordinary perceptual experi-

---

[1] He does of course experience a sense-datum which serves to *make* him aware of this object, but, as I have explained at length, he is not aware of the sense-datum as anything distinct from the object.

ences[1]—believing as I do that the phenomenalist's description of
them (so far as he gives any account at all of the nature of perceptual consciousness as distinct from the nature of physical
objects[2]) is simply incorrect. I can thus be said to have employed
the same 'empirical method' as that employed by Locke and
Hume, basing my conclusions on the observed character of my
own experiences, and going beyond this only to the extent that I
have taken it (as any philosopher has to) as a reliable guide to the
character of other people's experiences. I therefore disown the
title of 'metaphysician'.

I accept, then, not only the principle that all our knowledge
about the world is derived from experience and observation, but
even the principle that all our powers of understanding are so
derived. For this reason, though I have seen fit to speak of our
'innate' ability to interpret sense-data in terms of physical objects
—this signifying the fact that we do not and could not *learn by
experience* how to do so[3]—I have never spoken of 'the innate idea
of a physical object', which, as Locke witnessed, readily carries
the implication that a child possesses this 'idea' *before* it is first 'conveyed into his mind' by his senses. Where I depart from empiricism is in my view of the *character* of that class of our experiences
(our perceptual experiences) from which our understanding of
physical objects is derived—these experiences being constituted,
according to me, by an awareness of 'external' objects, with the
result that the understanding which we derive from them is an
understanding *of* something distinct from all possible experiences.[4]

It remains for me to sum up the main outcome of this discussion
by saying that there is less than no reason to reject the 'realist'

[1] Though I have, admittedly, for the purpose of explaining how it is that they
possess the character they do, had recourse to evolutionary theory, and have
described them partly in terms drawn from it (see above, pp. 88–90).

[2] See Section III, pp. 57–8. See also p. 119 below.

[3] And surely even Locke, despite his rejection of 'innate ideas', would have been
bound to agree that it is not on the strength of any experience that we refer our
sense-data to 'external' objects which they partially resemble.

[4] I depart from empiricism also in so far as I believe, not only that 'external'
objects fall within our understanding, but also that we have genuine knowledge of
their existence. But it is not with this latter departure that I am at present concerned
—this being discussed in Section V.

notion of physical objects on the particular ground that this notion could not possibly fall within our understanding.

I turn now to the second anti-realist argument that I wish to examine.

It has been said that if physical objects were something over and above all sense-data, then we could never teach a child the meaning of any word used to describe these objects. For we could never teach him to associate any such word with a class of objects distinct from anything of which he could have 'immediate experience'. The argument can be best put as follows. We can teach a child the meaning of such a word only by uttering the word in question at times when he is having an *experience* of a particular kind and by refraining from uttering it at any time when he is not having an experience of that kind. This being so, he could never learn to associate the word with a class of objects entirely distinct from all possible experiences.

I confess that I have never found this argument very convincing. My answer to it is simply this. Granted that the only way to teach a child the meaning of, for example, the word 'round' is to utter this word at such times as he is having an experience of a particular kind, the kind of experience in question is that of *being perceptually conscious of a round physical object*. And since, according to me, his having such an experience involves his being conscious of an object distinct from all possible experiences, there is no special difficulty in his learning to associate the word with a class of objects of this kind. Thus, while I am prepared to accept the premiss of the argument, I deny that the conclusion follows. It has seemed to follow only because it has been assumed at the outset that no account could be given of how a child comes in the first place to be aware of 'external' objects.

I should even venture to suggest that if the premiss be accepted, it actually presents difficulties for the phenomenalist which it does not present for me. For it is not at all clear to me what *his* answer is to the question: In teaching a child to associate a certain word with a certain class of physical objects, what kind of experience is it which he has to be having whenever we utter that word? If the answer is simply that he must on all such occasions be experiencing a sense-datum of a particular kind, then it is at least far from obvious how he comes to associate the word with a class of physical objects (i.e. on the phenomenalist view objects logically constructed from sense-data) as distinct from a class of sense-data. If, on the other hand, the phenomenalist takes the view, as I do, that the child must on all such occasions be perceptually conscious of a physical object of a particular kind, then I suggest that on his own view this is *not* just to have an experience of a particular kind. For if it is to involve something *besides* the experiencing of a sense-datum of a particular kind, then what this must be is the *taking for granted* that infinitely many other ones of particular kinds are obtainable. But there is certainly no kind of *experience* answering to this description which I have either ever had myself or can remotely imagine. If the expression 'taking for granted' means anything in this context, it denotes something in the nature of a *disposition* to act and feel in such a way as would be appropriate if all the relevant sense-data were obtainable.

I am not concerned to pursue further the difficulties which the phenomenalist encounters in this connection. It is sufficient to say that any account by a phenomenalist of how a child learns to associate words with physical objects would have to be considerably less straightforward than my own.

Having thus dealt with these two objections to *any* realist account of perception, I want now to discuss some further problems as they arise in connection with my own account.

I have spoken constantly of our innate capacity to interpret our visual and tactual sense-data *correctly* in terms of physical objects. And I have attempted to justify the use in this context of the word 'correctly'.[1] However, the question of whether a symbol has been interpreted correctly is not to be confused with the question of whether the information extracted from it is correct. There is no reason why we should not interpret a sense-datum or set of sense-data in accordance with the conventions of the sense-datum

[1] See pp. 87–90.

language and by so doing acquire a piece of false information. And this does on occasion happen: our senses sometimes *misinform* us. This is not, indeed, the only way in which we acquire false beliefs about the physical world. For, as I have explained at some length,[1] we learn *by experience* to extract more information from any given sense-datum or sense-data than would have been possible solely through our innate understanding of the sense-datum language, and in some cases the information extracted *by this means* is false. For example, we may mistake a pointed object in the far distance for the spire of a church. In such a case we have, in a clear sense, been misled by our past experience rather than by our senses. I repeat, however, that we are sometimes led into error merely by interpreting sense-data in accordance with the conventions of the sense-datum language. An extreme example of this is afforded by the case of a complete visual or tactual hallucination.

Now it is, in practice, always possible to detect such an error by experiencing further sense-data of appropriate kinds in addition to those on which the error is based. Thus there are various ways in which we can discover that we have been the victim of a hallucination. There is, however, certain special scientific evidence which suggests that the information supplied by our senses is *in general* lacking in accuracy—a lack which cannot be detected except by recourse to this evidence.

First, there is the straightforward evidence of the microscope that our senses always oversimplify the shapes of things. It seems, for instance, that almost any edge which looks completely straight to the naked eye, is really jagged. But further; we are told by the physicist that, contrary to what our senses would have us suppose, any object consists of a huge number of minute particles, and that a major proportion of the volume it appears to occupy is actually empty space.

It would, I think, generally be accepted that a microscope does indeed show that our (unaided) perception of shape is inexact. However, as regards the theory that objects are made up of discrete particles, many philosophers have held that if properly understood this in no way conflicts with the ordinary information

[1] Pp. 82–4.

of our senses. For they have held that these particles (which are never seen, even through a microscope) should be regarded not as *literally* composing physical objects, but as 'logically constructed' from the results which are or would be yielded by the relevant scientific tests—these results being, of course, within the reach of ordinary perception.

I am inclined myself to reject this view, largely because I distrust the motives of those who favour it. However, I should explain that I am extremely ignorant about scientific matters and am hardly in a position to say (a) how physicists themselves construe this theory of theirs and (b) how good would be the evidence for it were it taken at its face value—i.e. as not involving a 'logical construction'. What I *am* prepared to say is: that *if* there is good evidence for it even when so taken, the conclusion that our senses somewhat misrepresent the character of physical objects in no way threatens my account of perception. But before enlarging on this, I should mention briefly two well-known arguments purporting to show that this conclusion is untenable.

First, it is argued as follows. That which constitutes the evidence for any scientific discovery can itself be discovered only by means of the senses. Therefore, any alleged scientific discovery which calls in question the ordinary information of our senses is self-refuting; for the sole evidence on which it is reached is thereby itself called in question.

This argument does indeed show that the information of our senses cannot be regarded, on scientific grounds, as completely false in every respect. But no scientific theory actually involves this. And a theory is not self-refuting which *partially* undermines the information of our senses provided the evidence on which it is reached consists solely in certain such information *to the extent that this is still left intact*. Armstrong puts it well when he says: 'There is . . . nothing self-refuting in using selected deliverances of the senses to overthrow the other deliverances. . . . We would not be sawing off the branch we were sitting on, but sitting on a branch and sawing off the outermost part, the part on which we were *not* sitting'.[1]

[1] D. M. Armstrong, *Perception and the Physical World*, p. 167.

The second of these arguments would show, were it sound, that the information of our senses cannot be undermined by any scientific evidence whatever—not even that consisting of what is seen when an object is viewed through a microscope. The argument appeals to the way in which we do, and must, first learn the meaning of words describing physical objects. We learn their meaning through *ostensive definition*, that is, by hearing them uttered at times when we are confronted with the kinds of objects to which they apply. And we could, so it is said, learn their meaning in this way only if they really *did* apply to the objects in question. Thus, we can learn the meaning of 'completely straight' by hearing these words when confronted with such objects as footrules; and this presupposes that such objects are correctly described by means of these words. No scientific discovery, therefore, can possibly license the contrary conclusion. And the same applies to any attempt by science to undermine our ordinary descriptions of physical objects.

This argument is easily disposed of. To learn the meaning of words through ostensive definition is to hear them uttered at times when we are *perceptually conscious of* certain kinds of objects. And therefore, the success of our learning presupposes nothing about the *actual* character of the objects present at these times.

Neither of these arguments shows, therefore, that the information of our senses is immune to the findings of science.

Not even the physicist claims to have established that this information is totally false. The most his theories involve is its being somewhat imprecise, *schematic*. Compare, here, those diagrams of the brain, found in books on physiology, which we are warned are 'schematic and oversimplified'. They correctly schematize the spatial structure of the brain, without telling us of every individual cell. So too our senses, while not telling us of every particle composing the objects we perceive, correctly schematize the spatial structure of the physical world. And this schematic character of their information is, surely, exactly what we should have expected. For it is, after all, thanks to evolution that we are subjected in the way we are to the continual flow of information about our environment. And if evolutionary theory is correct, this information will be as precise, and no more so, as is necessary with a view to our survival. And I fancy that our prospects of longevity would be no better could we observe in perfect detail the shape, size and movements of every particle composing a piece of matter. On the contrary, I feel we should be so confused by the bewildering variety of our perceptual information that we should be unable to distinguish the important from the unimportant with a view to guiding our lives.

It is for this reason desirable (as well as inevitable) that we should for practical purposes ignore any discrepancies between the account of the world given by our senses and that given by science. Nor is it intellectually sinful for a philosopher to think of the former as an accurate account—any more than it is for a neurophysiologist to think of his diagrams as accurate portrayals of the brain. And therefore I shall, throughout the remainder of this book, freely speak of our senses as correctly informing us.

The time has come for me to consider the nature of the conventions governing the sense-datum language.

The first point to be made clear is that all of these are conventions solely for interpreting sense-data in terms of physical objects *of particular shapes, sizes and positions*. Once a child starts to interpret sense-data in accordance with conventions of this kind, through his innate capacity to do so, he can then learn *by experience* of all those other properties commonly ascribed to physical objects.

For a start, he can learn by experience how objects look, or otherwise 'appear', and thus ascribe to them properties of colour, smell, taste and the rest. Secondly, he can learn by experience of numerous 'dispositional' properties. For example, he can observe that objects of certain sorts break easily, and thus ascribe to them the property of fragility, that is the property of being 'disposed' to break. And to observe an object breaking is to observe two or more of its parts ceasing to occupy *positions* adjacent to one another. Again, he can observe that objects of certain sorts readily change their figure (that is their shape and size), while those of other sorts do not, and thus ascribe to them the properties of pliability or rigidity. He can in like manner learn of the causal properties of objects, what Locke called their 'powers'. He can observe, for example, that when objects of certain sorts are in close proximity to those of certain other sorts, the former invariably change their figure or cease to exist or move towards the latter; and by observing this he can ascribe to the latter the 'power' of changing the former's figure or of destroying or attracting it.

Sense-data, then—or rather visual and tactual sense-data—are governed by conventions whereby they symbolize the existence of objects having specific shapes, sizes and positions. Now, it should always be possible, at least in theory, to *formulate* the conventions by which any symbols are governed. And this must apply, therefore, to those governing sense-data. In actual practice, to formulate those governing tactual sense-data would, I think, be wholly unfeasible, since our language is ill-equipped to describe in sufficient detail the intrinsic characteristics of our sensations of touch. On the other hand, it is relatively well equipped to describe the coloured shapes in our visual field. And thus, to formulate the conventions governing visual sense-data might conceivably be practicable. Even here, however, the conventions are so numerous and complex that it would not be possible to formulate them in any measurable compass—certainly not within the scope of this book. I propose, none the less, to attempt the formulation of just one conventional rule, a fairly simple one, but which is fundamental to the interpretation of visual sense-data. And I shall, in addition, give some illustrations of the ways we extract information from these sense-data. I may hope, by these means, to cast some light both on the character of the sense-datum language in regard to visual sense-data—and indirectly in regard to tactual sense-data —and also on the interplay between our innate understanding of the sense-datum language and our ability to profit from experience.[1]

It is desirable, I feel, that my exposition be as brief and as simple as I can possibly make it. I hope, therefore, I may be forgiven if I indulge from time to time in minor oversimplifications. In particular, I shall omit mention of a number of qualifications

[1] See above, pp. 82-4.

which I deem inessential to my object, and which would make what I have to say less easy to follow.

I shall start with some preliminary remarks designed to prepare the ground for the formulation of the conventional rule just mentioned.

It must be kept in mind that in order to estimate the shape, size and position of a physical object with the greatest possible accuracy, we must examine it at a point close, though not too close, to our eyes. Only if we so examine it is our view of it (a) as detailed as possible and (b) perfectly stereoscopic.[1] This is well illustrated by reference to a sheet of corrugated iron. If we examine it either from too great or too short a distance, at best we cannot discern the irregularities in its surface with such precision, and at worst our view of it may be so imperfectly stereoscopic that it looks completely flat.

If, however, we are to have the best possible view of an object, distance is not the sole consideration. In the first place, our head must be facing more or less directly towards it, so that our view of it is constituted by a sense-datum more or less in the centre of our visual field. We must not, as we say, look at it 'out of the corner of our eye'. Secondly, the object itself must be so positioned that every part of its visible surface stands at approximately the same distance from our eyes—or as nearly so as its shape permits. That is to say, this surface must be viewed 'frontwards' rather than 'edgeways'. The surface of a sheet of corrugated iron serves, again, to highlight the importance of this.

Bearing these points in mind, let us first single out from all those visual sense-data which a person successively experiences those which (a) are situated more or less in the centre of his visual field and (b) are facing more or less directly forwards. (A sense-datum is naturally described as 'facing directly forwards' if every part of it is at approximately the *same depth* in our visual field. And it is a sense-datum of this kind that we experience while viewing an object's surface 'frontwards'.)

---

[1] The range of distances from our eyes within which objects are viewed in perfect stereoscopy is very small indeed. Professor Price has estimated that 'the upper limit is probably only a few feet, the lower some six inches'.

Now, anyone will discover that there is a certain depth or small range of depths d in his visual field such that, of those sense-data which we have thus singled out, the ones which he successively experiences at d are in general more highly differentiated, i.e. contain more detail, than those which he experiences at all other depths. (I say 'in general' since of course *some* sense-data which he experiences at d will be no more differentiated, or actually less so, than *some* of those which he experiences at other depths. For example, a sense-datum at d which constitutes his view of a stretch of concrete one foot away may well be less differentiated than one not at d which constitutes his view of a sheet of corrugated iron three feet away.)

There is, however, a qualification here which I think—despite what I said earlier—does call for attention. It is that if he *focuses his eyes* even onto an object a considerable distance away, his view of it will be more detailed than that of all the other objects (even those much nearer) which he can see simultaneously. In other words, any visual sense-datum, *whatever its depth*, which constitutes his view of an object onto which he focuses his eyes will be more differentiated than all the others which he experiences simultaneously. It remains true, nevertheless, that if he focuses them onto an object close though not too close to them, his view of it will be more detailed than that of an object *onto which he focuses them at some other time* situated either too far from them or too near them.

In order to allow for these considerations, what we have to do is to restrict still further those visual sense-data which we initially singled out from all those which a person successively experiences. Let us now single out those each of which satisfies the following *three* conditions: (a) it is situated more or less in the centre of his visual field, (b) it is facing more or less directly forwards and (c) it is more differentiated than all the others which he experiences simultaneously with it. Our original statement now holds good. Anyone will discover that there is a certain depth or small range of depths d in his visual field such that, of those sense-data which we have thus singled out, the ones which he successively experiences at d are in general more differentiated than those which he experiences at all other depths.

We are now in a position to formulate the conventional rule referred to above. What this rule states is that *any visual sense-datum at* d *which satisfies conditions* (*a*), (*b*) *and* (*c*) *is to symbolize the existence of a physical object one region of whose surface has the same shape as that possessed by this sense-datum.*[1]

The application of this rule is indispensable to all interpretation of visual sense-data in terms of physical objects. Plainly, however, it is not of itself sufficient to supply us with any but the scantiest information about the physical world. In order that our information may be more comprehensive, we must, in the first place, apply this rule in conjunction with further rules, and secondly, make use of our past experience to eke out that information extractable—by dint of our innate capacity—through the application of these rules alone. I cannot emphasize too strongly that innate capacity and experience are closely interlocked and perpetually supplement one another throughout the continued process of perceptual discovery.

The further conventional rules are, as I have indicated, enormously complicated and not susceptible of formulation within the compass of this book, if at all. But I think that it will be helpful to examine shortly the character of those visual sense-data to which these rules are applicable.

They apply not to any sense-data taken individually, but rather to certain sequences of sense-data. The character of these can most easily be got across to the reader by a reference to the circumstances in which anyone experiences such a sequence.

The diagram below represents some region of the surface of a

---

[1] If the reader be in doubt about the meaning here of the words 'same shape', I can illustrate this by inviting him to imagine he is manipulating a ball of plasticine into a variety of shapes. Into whatever shape he were to transform its front surface (that part at which he was looking), his visual field would contain a colour-patch having the *same shape* as was possessed by this surface. Thus, when this surface was rectangular and flat—like the side of a match-box—his visual field would contain a rectangular and flat colour-patch. Likewise, when it was rectangular but uneven —like the surface of a sheet of corrugated iron—his visual field would contain a rectangular but uneven colour-patch. Or, when it was round but curved—like one half of the surface of a golf-ball—his visual field would contain a round but curved colour-patch.

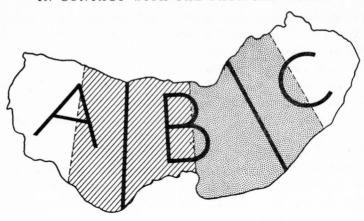

physical object[1] which is such that one cannot see the whole of it simultaneously, or at any rate one cannot have an optimum view (as characterized above[2]) of the whole of it. This region is divided (arbitrarily) into three sub-regions, A, B and C, such that one *can* see simultaneously—and have an optimum view of—the whole of any *one* of them, and also both the whole of the shaded area comprising part of A and part of B and the whole of the dotted area comprising part of B and part of C. Suppose, now, that the object to which this region belongs is placed just in front of us in such a way that we can, by making suitable movements of our eyes (or if need be our body), scan the entire region in question from, let us say, left to right. By doing this, we can experience a set of five successive sense-data having the same shapes as those possessed respectively by (i) A, (ii) the shaded area, (iii) B, (iv) the dotted area and (v) C—each of these sense-data being, moreover, at the optimum depth[3] and satisfying the three conditions of (a) being situated more or less in the centre of our visual field, (b) facing more or less directly forwards and (c) being more differentiated than any others we experience simultaneously with it. We experience, therefore, a sequence of sense-data each individual

---

[1] It is immaterial whether it be thought of as representing a region which is or which is not completely flat (i.e. which has two dimensions or three).

[2] P. 125.

[3] That is, the depth *d* as defined above.

member of which is amenable to the conventional rule that I have formulated. Thus, suppose that their shapes are respectively s_1, s_2, s_3, s_4 and s_5, and that the times at which we experience them are respectively t_1, t_2, t_3, t_4 and t_5. Then, by applying this rule, we can discover that at t_1 there exists a physical object one region of whose surface has the shape s_1, that at t_2 there exists a physical object one region of whose surface has the shape s_2, and so on. Now in order that we may apply the *further* conventional rules to the sequence taken as a whole, the latter must be of such a form as I may describe by saying that each of the sense-data 'merges into' the succeeding one so as to produce an uninterrupted flow of visual experience. My meaning should be clear if I say that the sequence must be such as we should experience if we passed our eyes over the region A/B/C in one continuous motion from left to right. Roughly speaking, what occurs is this. To begin with, the first of the five sense-data—i.e. that having the shape s_1—changes its position in our visual field or the direction in which it faces[1] in such a way as to 'make room for' the second sense-datum—i.e. that having the shape s_2, this consisting of *part of the first sense-datum* together with a further sense-datum. Then, this second sense-datum changes *its* position or direction in such a way as to 'make room for' the third sense-datum—i.e. that having the shape s_3, this consisting of part of the second sense-datum together with yet a further sense-datum. And so on until we end up with the fifth sense-datum—i.e. that having the shape s_5.

As I have said, by interpreting each of these sense-data separately in accordance with the primary rule formulated above,

[1] A visual sense-datum is naturally described as 'changing its direction' if it undergoes some change in respect of the *relative depths* in our visual field of different parts of it (cf. H. H. Price, *Perception*, p. 218). Thus, if every part of it is initially at the same depth (i.e. it is facing 'directly forwards'), it may be said to change its direction if it so changes its precise position in our visual field that some parts of it are then at a greater depth than others. And, if it then further changes its position in such a way that the *difference in depth* between its deepest and its least deep parts either increases or decreases, it may be said to have undergone yet a further change in its direction.

As for the need to include here the words 'or the direction in which it faces', this can clearly be seen if we picture the sequence of sense-data that we experience when we walk all round the exterior of a house.

we discover the existence of five regions possessing respectively these five shapes. By applying the further rules to the sequence as a whole, we discover thereby, first, the fact that five such regions *all belong to a single object*, and secondly, that they *overlap* one another in a certain way, namely as indicated in the diagram, to form a composite region of a certain shape. And hence, we discover the existence of a physical object one continuous region of whose surface has this latter shape.[1]

It is not quite true to say that we can discover this *merely* by applying these rules. For it is only in experiencing the final member of the sequence that we reach this discovery, and accordingly it involves the assumption of a physical surface preserving a constancy throughout the period of the entire sequence (i.e. the period from t_1 to t_5) in the shapes of all its adjacent parts. And we are only in a position to make this assumption on the basis of our past experience, which has taught us to associate visual sense-data possessing certain detailed characteristics with physical objects possessing certain properties including that of stability in respect of shape. Roughly, we have found in the past that we have consistently been able to *reverse* specific sequences of visual sense-data (i.e. by moving our eyes or body in the opposite direction to that in which we just *have* moved them) without detecting any change in the shapes of the members composing them.[2]

My next step is to say that wherever, in the preceding paragraphs, I have used the expression 'a physical object', this expression should be taken as denoting either what would normally be regarded as a separate object or what would normally be regarded as a *composite* object, that is an object constituted by a set of adjoining objects and having a single composite surface. Once this

[1] It will be seen that the form of procedure which I have described enables us equally to discover the existence of an object whose surface *as a whole* has some particular shape. Thus, once we have interpreted any given sequence of visual sense-data in terms of a surface of a given shape, we can always know, by dint of what that shape is, whether it is possessed by the whole or by one region only of an object's surface, there being no shape possessable by both.

[2] The significance of the word 'reverse' is, of course, that if a sequence is repeated a number of times, only each time in the reverse order to that of the previous time, this enables the several occurrences of it to form between them a single uninterrupted sequence.

is understood, it is apparent that the manner whereby we discover such a composite surface is the same in principle[1] as that whereby we discover the surface of a separate object.

It is basically an arbitrary matter how we determine what are to be treated as separate objects. I suggest, however, that in common parlance a given part of any composite object would most naturally be described as one separate object if (a) it can readily be moved[2] in relation to the remainder of the composite object, that is if its spatial relationship thereto can readily be altered, and (b) no part of *it* can readily be moved in relation to the remainder of itself. And such movability can be categorized as a 'dispositional' property, discoverable by experience in the general manner that I indicated above.[3]

Having said this, it remains for me to point out that once we have discovered a composite object of any given shape, and have determined which of its parts are to be treated as separate objects, we then have at our disposal all the information we require in order to know both the relative sizes[4] and the relative positions of these separate objects.

The ways in which our innate capacity to interpret visual sense-data is supplemented by past experience are of untold variety and complexity. To take an instance, we can learn by experience to extract all manner of information from sense-data other than those at the optimum depth, so that we can, for example, estimate with a considerable degree of accuracy the shapes, sizes and positions

---

[1] This qualification is obviously an important one, particularly if we consider that the whole earth is a composite object, and that it is plainly impracticable to scan its entire surface in one uninterrupted motion. I must therefore refer the reader to my remark in connection with this point in the paragraph below concerning our use of past experience.

[2] How readily? Are we allowed, for example, to use mechanical aids or tools, e.g. pliers or scissors? All that can be said is that generally speaking, the *more* easily it can be moved, the more willing we are to regard it as a separate object. (Is a floor-board a separate object?)

[3] Pp. 123-4.

[4] We should note that in specifying 'the size' of an object by the assignment of numerical values—by saying, for example, that it is eight inches long and six inches wide—we are in effect *comparing* the extent of its dimensions with the length of a given part of some standard measuring instrument (in this case a foot-rule).

of objects at all distances from our eyes.[1] Again, we can learn by experience to relate the information extracted from sense-data at one time to that extracted from them at any previous time even if the flow of our visual experience has been interrupted between these times, e.g. by sleep or even by the act of closing our eyes for a moment. Many other instances come to mind. Clearly I cannot undertake here an exhaustive classification of the multifarious processes involved.

So far as tactual sense-data are concerned, we acquire information through our innate capacity aided by past experience in a manner comparable to that in which we do so by means of visual sense-data, though the conventional rules we apply to them are very different. Thus we may ascertain the surface of an object (or set of adjoining objects) by undergoing a sequence of tactual sense-data whose character I can only convey by saying that it is what we experience when we run, say, our finger over all of that surface.

Finally, our experience gives rise to associations, on the one hand, between visual sense-data and tactual sense-data, and on the other, between these sense-data and ones belonging to the other senses, thus enabling us to extract information about physical objects from sounds, smells or tastes.

[1] Obviously, this statement needs to be qualified in the case of objects at a very great distance, such as aeroplanes or stars.

V

CONCERNING THE JUSTIFICATION OF OUR BELIEFS ABOUT THE PHYSICAL WORLD

In the preceding section I have set forth an account of the manner in which our perceptual experiences afford us an awareness of 'external' objects. This account involves a repudiation of two widely accepted doctrines of *empiricism*, viz. (i) that the notion of 'external' objects—in Hume's phrase, objects 'specifically different from our perceptions'—could not possibly fall within our understanding and (ii) that even if it did, there could be no possible ground for believing that any such objects actually exist. I have already stated my reasons for thinking that the first of these doctrines is false.[1] I have now to explain why I equally reject the second of them.

It will be observed that this further doctrine only comes into play on the basis that the first is ill-founded, i.e. on the basis that 'external' objects *do* fall within our understanding. For this reason doubtless, it has received relatively little separate attention from philosophers, and its truth has been asserted rather than supported by any detailed argument. It is not easy to meet such an assertion save by counter-assertion. But I shall endeavour to show that a contrary view can be upheld.

I can find no better statement of the principle on which this doctrine appears to be founded than in a remark by Professor Ayer on the subject of *inductive reasoning*. Having first explained that he uses this expression 'to cover all the cases in which we pass from a particular statement of fact, or set of particular statements of fact, to a factual conclusion which they do not formally [i.e. logically] entail', he proceeds to make the following pronouncement.

'In *all* such reasoning [my italics] we make the assumption that there is a measure of uniformity in nature; or, roughly speaking,

[1] Pp. 106–18.

that the future will, in the appropriate respects, resemble the past. We think ourselves entitled to treat the instances which we have been able to examine as reliable guides to those that we have not.'[1]

Now I have never suggested (quite the contrary) that we come by our beliefs about the physical world through any process of *reasoning*—i.e. through any conscious 'passage' from facts about our experience to facts about 'external' objects. And therefore this pronouncement of Ayer's is wholly consistent with my account in the previous section of how we do come by these beliefs. Nevertheless, I am prepared to admit that if this pronouncement were correct, it would follow that these beliefs cannot be said to have any *rational foundation*. For I am willing to allow, at least for the sake of argument, that a belief in the existence of 'external' objects could not be regarded as rational were it not even *capable* of being supported by any resort to reasoning;[2] and clearly it could not be so supported if the only form of 'factual' (i.e. non-deductive) reasoning were such as is based on assumptions about the 'uniformity of nature'. No assumptions of this kind could possibly entitle us to make any inference from the character of our experience to the existence of something outside our experience.

But I do not accept that this pronouncement *is* correct. I am not concerned to catalogue forms of reasoning. All I shall do is to point out one particular form the validity of which would be generally accepted and which, I suggest, carries no implication of the uniformity of nature. And I shall argue that it can be employed to lend at least very considerable support to the existence of an external world.

The form of reasoning in question is that on which anyone tacitly relies who engages in the operation of deciphering a complex code. This operation consists in the discovery, maybe through

---

[1] A. J. Ayer, *The Problem of Knowledge*, Penguin ed. p. 72, Macmillan ed. p. 77.

[2] I say that I allow this 'for the sake of argument' since it may involve a misapprehension of what is implied by describing a belief as 'rational'. Ideally, what is called for is a thorough analysis of the meaning both of this word and also of allied words such as 'reasonable', 'valid', 'justified'. However, such an analysis, to be worthwhile, would require a whole volume to itself, and must therefore here be forgone.

a lengthy process of trial and error, of a 'key', or method of interpretation, which enables one to extract information from what would otherwise be a meaningless set of markings—or, in some cases, of sounds. That is to say, one discovers that if one attaches a given significance to each different marking or sound, the complete set yields a meaningful and coherent piece of information. Given this discovery, one has no hesitation in concluding, first, that these markings or sounds are indeed the symbols of a code and secondly, that they possess the particular significance thus attached to them. And the reasoning which underlies this conclusion is, simply, that the only alternative would be to suppose a *coincidence*[1] too extravagant to be contemplated.

Doubtless the thoroughgoing empiricist would insist that it is only through past experience that one is in a position to judge what would and would not involve a coincidence. Thus, he would hold that experience, and experience alone, can establish the unlikelihood of anything *not* serving to encode information being nevertheless amenable to some complex principle of 'decipherment' as though it did so serve. If this were so, then even the form of reasoning here cited would rely on the assumption that nature is in a certain respect uniform, viz. in respect of the rarity of such 'accidental' decipherability. But not only do I find this inherently unplausible. It seems to me that the very assumption of the uniformity of nature *itself* involves an appeal to the notion of coincidence. To take the simplest possible example, in assuming that because in the past lightning has always been followed by thunder, the same will hold good in the future, are we not implicitly appealing to the fact that the past regularity of this phenomenon would be too great a coincidence were it not the manifestation of an *immutable law of nature*?[2]

---

[1] The question how the notion of 'coincidence' is to be defined is both interesting and difficult. But it is not possible to discuss this here.

[2] I might point out that even Hume—the person largely responsible for the favoured view of the nature of factual reasoning—allows himself, in discussing the 'constant conjunction' of 'impressions' and 'ideas', to remark: 'Such a constant conjunction, in such an infinite number of instances, can never arise *from chance*' (my italics). In other words, to suppose that it did so arise would be to suppose too improbable a coincidence.

I submit, therefore, that the form of reasoning involved in the deciphering of a code is *not* based on any assumption about the uniformity of nature, yet is one which all of us would freely endorse. Let me illustrate its operation by means of a simple example.

Suppose that one finds a tree incised with elaborate markings. It is possible that these have been made by an animal or by the ravages of time. But it is also possible that they have been made deliberately to serve as the symbols of some code. Now suppose that one hits on some method of interpretation the application of which makes the totality of these markings yield a coherent piece of information. And suppose that the method of interpretation and the resulting information are together of such a character that the possibility of this result being due to chance is infinitely remote. In that case one is amply justified in concluding that one has indeed deciphered a code.

It seems to me that this very same form of reasoning can be employed in connection with our sense-data. Intrinsically, these are mere items of experience which do not point the way to anything beyond themselves.[1] On the other hand, if they are treated as symbols and interpreted in the manner I have sought to describe, then they yield a coherent and detailed view of an entire complex of physical objects. And this result, surely, could not be accountable to chance. It cannot be for no reason that our successive sense-data are of *just* those kinds which, when so interpreted, produce such a result.

Now of course, once we have succeeded in deciphering any complex code, and have satisfied ourselves that it *is* a code, we are still left with the question whether the information it contains is or is not *correct* information. And we may well not be in a position to assume that it *is* correct without recourse to independent

---

[1] Furthermore, I can attach no sense to saying, as some phenomenalists have done, that suitable groups of successive visual or tactual sense-data can be *fitted together in the mind*—by an activity of what Professor Price calls 'spatial synthesis' (vide *Perception*, pp. 217–18)—to form 'pictures' of the complete surfaces of physical objects. Obviously, one cannot construct a composite *image* of such a surface—the surface, say, comprising all six sides of a match-box. And I fail to comprehend what other mental activity could here be envisaged.

corroboration. But in the case of the information we extract from sense-data, no such corroboration can be forthcoming. However this case is, in an important respect, unique. If we discover, say, that a set of markings on a tree contain information, there is an obvious reason why this information *may* be false. These markings must have been made by a human being, and there is always a live possibility of any human being communicating false information. On the other hand, whatever reason might be adduced for the falsity of the information contained in our sense-data, plainly it could not be this one. The question, therefore, is whether *any* reason could be given which is both intelligible[1] and worthy of serious contemplation. If in fact none could—and I can myself think of none—then the confidence which all of us repose in the existence of a physical world can be said to be rational.

I feel that I should be biting off more than I could chew were I to pursue this question, since I could set about this only by listing every conceivable suggestion that any sceptic might put forward and attempting to give reasons why each of them in turn may be discounted. So I shall simply say, in conclusion, that if I am at all right in my account of how we interpret our sense-data, it seems to me that their amenability to this interpretation points very strongly to the existence of a physical world and that the onus is on anyone who disputes this to give a sound and sensible reason for doing so.

---

[1] I am emboldened to suggest that the idea, put forward by Descartes, that there might be a malignant demon bent on instilling false beliefs in us—who could, therefore, be the source of this information—is *not* intelligible.

VI

THE CONCEPT OF PERCEIVING

I have now set forth my views as to the character of our perceptual experiences; and I have defended these views against what I take to be the most likely objections to them. There is, however, a residual problem which I have not yet touched on. It is one which arises from the following considerations.

In order for it to be true that a given object is perceived, it is not required of this object that it look, or otherwise appear, in all respects as it is. A straight stick partly in water is seen no less on account of its looking bent. Nor is it seen any less by one who mistakenly believes that it is really bent. Such a person will think, and may say, that he sees a bent stick; but in thinking or saying this he will be wrong, since what he actually sees is a straight stick. Similarly, if a coat on the floor is misidentified as a dog, this does not preclude the misidentifier from seeing it: though he thinks he sees a dog, what he actually sees is a coat. Not only may one be mistaken as to the character of what one sees; one may even be mistaken as to its location. If one wanders absentmindedly through one's garden, one may see the tree which stands in one part of it, yet take it for the tree in some other part of it. Nor is one exempt from error as to the position of what one sees in relation to one's own body. One may gaze into an invisible mirror and think what one sees is in front of one while actually it is behind one. It is even possible to see some object while thinking one is seeing none. The taker of mescalin may think he is hallucinated at a moment he is not. The student of psychology may think he sees only an after-image when really what he sees is an object. In short, the mere fact that one sees a given object involves far less than might at first have been supposed. And the same (or similar) points hold good for the remaining four senses. The notion, therefore, of perceiving an object becomes a somewhat puzzling one. What is there to be said about it of a positive nature? What exactly is required for the truth of a statement to the effect that a given object is perceived by a given person? It is this question that I am going now to discuss.

It seems clear, for a start, that it is impossible to perceive anything without experiencing a sense-datum. But the mere fact that one experiences a sense-datum, and that it possesses a certain character, is consistent with the fact either that one perceives no object at all or that one does perceive any object from an infinite range. Evidently, in order for it to be true that one perceives a given object, the object in question must stand to one's sense-datum in a certain relationship. If this relationship obtains, then one does in fact perceive that object regardless of what one thinks one perceives and regardless of the character of the sense-datum. The task before me is to specify this relationship.

It has often been maintained that one cannot be said to perceive a given object unless that object is partly responsible for the causation of one's sense-datum.[1] I believe this is correct. It has, I think, been conclusively argued by Mr. H. P. Grice.

Suppose [he says] that it looks to X as if there is a clock on the shelf; what more is required for it to be true to say that X sees a clock on the shelf? There must, one might say, actually be a clock on the shelf which is in X's field of view. . . . But this does not seem to be enough. For it is logically conceivable that there should be some method by which an expert could make it look to X as if there were a clock on the shelf on occasions when the shelf was empty: there might be some apparatus by which X's cortex could be suitably stimulated, or some technique analogous to post-hypnotic suggestion. If such treatment were applied to X on an occasion when there actually was a clock on the shelf, and if X's impressions [i.e. sense-data] were found to continue unchanged when the clock was removed or its position altered, then I think we should be inclined to say that X did not see the clock which was before his eyes, just because we should regard the clock as

1 See Section IV, p. 79.

playing no part in the origination of his impression. Or, to leave the realm of fantasy, it might be that it looked to me as if there were a certain sort of pillar in a certain direction at a certain distance, and there might actually be such a pillar in that place; but if, unknown to me, there were a mirror interposed between myself and the pillar, which reflected a numerically different though similar pillar, it would certainly be incorrect to say that I saw the first pillar, and correct to say that I saw the second; and it is extremely tempting to explain this linguistic fact by saying that the first pillar was, and the second was not, causally irrelevant to the way things looked to me.[1]

But this takes us only part of the way. For the causal process which brings about one's sensory experience involves many objects other than the object one is said to perceive. A distinction has been drawn by Professor Price between what he calls the 'standing' and the 'differential' conditions of a sense-datum. 'There are', he says, 'certain conditions which condition *all* the sense-data of any one sense, conditions in the absence of which none of them can come into being: in the case of visual sense-data, there must be a source of light, an eye, a retina, an optic nerve, etc., and these must be in a certain state. There must also be a diaphanous medium. But these standing conditions, just because they are necessary to all the visual sense-data alike, do not wholly determine any one of them. For that, something more is wanted, a varying or differential condition which accounts for the difference between this red sense-datum and that blue one, between this square one and that elliptical one.'[2] The suggestion is that one sees a given object if and only if that object constitutes the *differential* condition of one's visual sense-datum; and *mutatis mutandis* for the other senses.[3]

[1] H. P. Grice, 'The Causal Theory of Perception', *Aristotelian Society Supplementary Proceedings*, 1961, p. 142. This paper was reprinted in *Perceiving, Sensing, and Knowing*, ed. R. J. Swartz (*vide* pp. 461–2).

[2] H. H. Price, *Perception*, p. 70.

[3] I ought to mention that Price himself finally accepts this suggestion only with a certain reservation. But this need not concern us, since it has to do with his own account of what a physical object is.

But I do not think this will suffice.

Consider first Price's examples of the *standing* conditions of visual sense-data. 'There must', he says, 'be a source of light, an eye, a retina, an optic nerve, etc., and these must be in a certain state.' But while it is true that these must be in one of a certain range of states, their precise state both varies constantly and contributes importantly to the character of one's visual sense-data at any given moment. The idea is, perhaps, that one is not said to see these objects just because they are always involved *in some one way or other* in the causal processes which terminate in any of one's visual experiences. But if this is the point, it is not then clear why these examples of 'standing' conditions should include the source of light. For though, as Price says, there must be *some* source of light, no one given source is always involved in such causal processes; for what provides the source at any given time may be any one of a large range of different objects. It may be the sun, but it may also be an electric light, a torch, a fire, a match. And further, what it is will be causally relevant to the character of one's visual sense-data. If it is an object which emits blue light, then all one's visual sense-data will be blue; if it is a very dim light, then all of them will be dark and lacking in the usual irregularities of shape. And if the light it emits is what we call 'normal', this fact is still causally relevant to the character of these sense-data. It is, therefore, at least not obvious why whatever it is should not be described as conditioning these *differentially*. Yet we do not want to say that it is necessarily seen: it may be concealed for instance, or what one does see (by means of its light) may be in a different direction from it. The same difficulty arises with Price's final example of a 'standing' condition—the presence of a 'diaphanous medium'. No one such medium conditions all one's visual sense-data, since what constitutes this medium varies from one moment to the next. It may be this set of air particles, it may be that set; and it may or may not include a transparent object of any single kind whatever. And what it does include will be causally relevant to the character of one's visual sense-data. It may include, say, a type of glass which distorts either the shape, the colour or both of everything seen through it.

Yet we do not say that it is itself necessarily seen. Air particles are invisible, and so is any glass whose transparency is perfect.

It might conceivably be possible to define a 'differential condition' in such a way as to overcome these difficulties. But even if this were achieved, I do not think it would solve our problem. For I think it is essential to the notion of perceiving an object that the object in question help bring about one's experience in a particular sort of way. Should it contribute to this in any other sort of way, then, regardless of the extent of its contribution, one does not perceive it. If, for example, one receives a blow on the back of the head, and undergoes as a result the experience known as 'seeing stars', one does not see the object with which this blow is delivered. It is tempting to say that the reason one does not see it is that no light-rays are transmitted from it to one's eyes. And this is, I think, very much to the point. Yet it must somehow be possible to define the notion of seeing an object without any mention of such things as light-rays. For one is fully able to employ this notion who knows nothing of optical science. It was employed indeed, and in the very same way as it now is, long before light-rays were even discovered. The point is this. The precise chain of events involved in our seeing an object is what it is, and as science discovered it to be, only by dint of our physiological constitution. Had evolution progressed by a different route, the mechanism whereby we see might have been a very different one. It will not do, therefore, to define the notion of seeing in such a way as restricts the possibilities of what this mechanism might have turned out to be. But I think it is possible, without doing this, to state a requirement which any conceivable chain of events would have to meet in order to constitute the seeing of an object. (I shall discuss seeing separately before I pass to the perceiving of objects through the other senses.)

At the beginning of this section, I cited some cases where one sees a certain object while taking it for something else. The frequency of such cases has been stressed by Mr Warnock in a paper on this topic;[1] and I am much indebted to all that he says in it.

[1] G. J. Warnock, 'Seeing', *Proceedings of the Aristotelian Society*, 1954-55. Reprinted in *Perceiving, Sensing, and Knowing*, ed. R. J. Swartz.

But of special significance is a qualification that he made in a postscript added later.[1] He abides by the fact that to see a given object does not require that it be correctly identified, or even that it be identified as any object at all.[2] But he suggests, I think rightly, that it does require 'at least some ability to pick out and identify objects' even if one does not, on a given occasion, exercise this ability 'correctly or even at all'. Some blind men, he says, who become 'able to see' through surgical operation, 'remain permanently unable to make any *use* of vision', and 'in such cases it seems natural to say that . . . they never become able to see *things* at all'. And the position may be comparable for the new born infant. To use my own terminology, although such persons experience visual sense-data, they are unable to 'interpret' them to identify physical objects, and are debarred thereby from being said to 'see' them.

This brings us, I think, to the essential point about the seeing of objects. One is said, first, to have the general ability to see objects if one is able, through interpreting one's visual sense-data in the manner I described in Section IV, to acquire correct information about the physical world. Thanks to evolution, we are endowed (most of us) with a complex physiological mechanism whereby this is achieved. In general, whenever some object contributes by means of it to the experiencing of a visual sense-datum, we become apprised thereby of the existence and character of that object—and are therefore said to see it. But this mechanism, like most mechanisms designed for a particular purpose, falls short of total perfection. Sometimes, when a certain object helps bring about a sense-datum in the very same manner, we extract from the sense-datum some false information. Nevertheless, since our mechanism of seeing was still involved, and since it operated in the normal way, it is allowed to be said that this object was (in fact) 'seen'. That is, someone other than the percipient who knows what the object really was—or the percipient himself on a subsequent occasion—finds it natural to say this.

My suggestion, in short, is roughly this. A given person sees

---

[1] *Perceiving, Sensing, and Knowing*, pp. 66–7.
[2] Compare my own example of an object which is taken for an after-image.

a given object if the mode of causal relationship between it and his visual sense-datum is such that, *in general*, when any object is related in this way to any of his visual sense-data, he becomes visually conscious of a physical object of the kind that this object actually is. What precisely this relationship is must be discovered by the scientist. In other words, it is for him to discover by what precise causal mechanism our visual experiences afford us—for the most part—an awareness of the physical world and as it really is.

There arises one minor objection. We can be said to see an object notwithstanding the presence of a 'diaphanous medium' which distorts its appearance, and which would, moreover, distort the appearance of *any* object seen through it. It cannot be said, therefore, that we should *in general* see any object as it is in cases where this medium was involved in the causal nexus between an object and our experience. The same applies if our vision is distorted through some ocular or other physiological abnormality. There are two points to be made here. First, when any such factor is present, we can usually know both that it *is* present and in what systematic ways it brings about its distorting effects. We are able, therefore, mentally to discount these effects. Secondly, just suppose that our vision were continuously distorted—as the result, say, of an eye injury—and that we remained for a time unaware of this fact. While we should always err about the character of any object, we should do so systematically. And provided this error were not excessive, we could still be credited with the ability to see things. Quite simply: an ability that is impaired need not be said to be lacking altogether.

I now turn briefly to non-visual perception.

The above definition of the seeing of an object would appear, with the appropriate verbal changes, to hold equally good for feeling. That is, a given person feels a given object if the mode of causal relationship between it and his tactual sense-datum is such that, in general, when any object is related in this way to any of his tactual sense-data, he becomes tactually conscious of the kind of object that this object actually is.

The case is slightly different, though still very similar, with the remaining three senses. If I am at all right so far, the notions both of seeing and feeling an object are inseparable from those of being visually and tactually *conscious* of it; and this seems as it should be. But, as I noted in Section IV,[1] our other senses barely (if at all) make us conscious of physical objects. We often talk of *inferring* an object's presence from a sound or a smell, or the presence of some ingredient in a food from its taste. Still, just as the seeing or feeling of objects requires a general ability to be visually or tactually conscious of them, so I think that the hearing, smelling or tasting of them requires a general ability to make this kind of inference. Take, for example, our sense of smell. When an object is related in a certain causal fashion to an olfactory sense-datum, it is frequently possible for its presence to be inferred from that sense-datum alone. And the performance of this inference is said to constitute the smelling of this object. But such inferences are fallible. An olfactory sense-datum may be produced by an object via the same causal mechanism, yet the person experiencing it misidentify the object.[2] But because this mechanism is still involved, the object in question is allowed to count as what in fact is smelt.

The foregoing account is doubtless oversimplified. There may be many refinements in our daily use of verbs of perception that I have left out of account. But I have sought to bring to light the fundamental principles.

[1] P. 104.

[2] Alternatively, of course, he may identify it correctly but without any help from this olfactory sense-datum—say by seeing it simultaneously. Or he may be at a loss to identify it at all.

INDEX

N 68 JD

Pennyauik